ZEN EDGE

ALEXANDER ELIOT *Zen Edge*

Introduction by Taitetsu Unno

A CONTINUUM BOOK • THE SEABURY PRESS • NEW YORK

The Seabury Press
815 Second Avenue
New York, New York 10017

First American edition 1979
Copyright © 1976 by Alexander Eliot
Introduction Copyright © 1979 by The Seabury Press, Inc.

LIBRARY OF CONGRESS CATALOGING IN PUBLICATION DATA

Eliot, Alexander.   Zen edge.
1. Spiritual life (Zen Buddhism)
2. Eliot, Alexander. I. Title.
BQ9288.E43   1979   294.3'4'40924 [B]   78-21701
ISBN 0-8164-9355-3

For the woman with the *Koto*

Introduction

AMONG the current crop of books on Zen in Western languages, primarily English, some serious and others frivolous, very few give the real taste of Zen. The majority, it seems, have more the stink of Zen in varying concentrations, whether the product is the work of a scholar, *roshi,* popularizer, translator, convert, or sometime practitioner. They are all discolored by some form of egoism, whether personal, cultural, racial, or religious. While the taste of Zen may be difficult to explain precisely, being a subtle but vivid perception, it is a kind of cleansing experience—the shorning of artificialities, the freeing of passions in pure form, the joyful lightening of body and mind.

Alexander Eliot's *Zen Edge* has the impalpable taste of Zen. The author is not trying to sell, defend, compare, or appropriate Zen in any way, nor is he out to prove a point, earn merit, or use it for any personal purpose. Rather, what he does is to lay bare his deepest yearnings, his hidden secrets, his sensitivity to love, hate, and death, struggling to enter what he calls "the central dilemma, Man himself, and deal with that creatively." Naturally, then, this book is not about dogma or dogmatics of any particular religion, nor is it an advocacy for either the Easterner or Westerner. The book does not provide fast and easy answers, as some so-called Zen works purport to do, regarding perplexing questions of human existence, but it does explore in all its fascinating dimensions what it means to be truly human—the felt pain and joy, the confusion and exhilaration, the tragic and comic.

While ranging over many questions and issues, interspersed with personal reflections and choice vignettes, the book is unified by an optimistic expectation for the future of humanity: "East, West, North, South, wherever one may look today, one sees new beginnings of such joyous work and infinitely difficult play. We can witness the budding of planetary consciousness. Not only that, but partake in it." Such a hope is evident in a number of people, including the author himself, who appear in the book: the distinguished Japanese philosopher Keiji Nishitani, the Catholic theologian Professor Guardini; the highly respected lay teacher of Zen, Masao Abe; the Reverend Song Ryong Hearn, the author's first *kalyāna-mitra;* and the monk of Mt. Athos, whose final gesture is memorably graphic. In the words of Eliot, "I stood dripping on the shore of time, and Simon waved to me from eternity."

These men are not interested in proclaiming the superiority of one path or doctrine over others or, going to the other extreme, of advocating a universal religion of salvation by erasing all diversities. Nor are they simply opting for spirituality over materiality, for the forces of good over evil. Rather, they have plunged deeply into the heart of existence itself, into fundamental subjectivity, into "the freedom of inmost withinness"; each has an experience and knowledge of something profoundly human, which draws out from those whom they touch a gentle concern and deep compassion for all of life.

When such people speak or write, reality comes attached with their words, and people who have ears to hear will also awaken to the selfsame reality in themselves and in the world. Nāgārjuna, a third-century Buddhist thinker, called such words *deśanā,* "illuminating teaching," in contrast to words disconnected from any form of reality, internal or external, which he designated as *prapañca,* "word-play." Buddhism has a high regard for the proper use of language, for that is a unique vehicle of enlightenment that only human beings are blessed with, but it harshly rejects words devoid of reality and sincerity, manipulated by those in power to control people in countless subtle and not so subtle ways.

The author may not be familiar with such technical distinctions, but what he expresses in this book moves in the direction of *deśanā,* for he is unafraid to live with the reality of his soul: "I wish to dance with a differing drum. Namely, the heart, whether it hurts or leaps for joy as the case may be. One hand clapping, in short." This leads him consciously or unconsciously to saying the *nembutsu,* calling on the name of the Buddha of Light, a time-honored practice of the Pure Land tradition of other power, as he exerts himself in the grand affirmation of sitting meditation, the opposite extreme of self power. An absurd contradiction, so the dogmatists will say, of combining these divergent paths within Buddhism; but going beyond the doctrinaire distinctions (which are parts of lifeless objectivity) into the heart of what it means to be truly human, one shares in the fundamental insight: to suffer pain and grief, yet through grace live through them with dignity and gratefulness.

Throughout the exalted Buddhist tradition, the Buddha of Light shines in the darkness, focusing on human suffering, transforming it into joy, and nurturing new life. In the *Eternal Smile,* Par Lagerkvist, from a different angle, puts it precisely thus:

> "One must take pains seriously over joy. A man should bury his grief in an ocean of light; everyone will see that all the light is streaming from this one little grief, as if from a luminous gem, wrenched with toil out of the dark mountains."

Nāgārjuna, the philosopher, expressed this according to his own logic: *samsara* is no different from nirvana, and nirvana is no different from samsara.

Zen Edge is a felicitous title, for in one sense the book is on the edge or fringe of Japanese Zen with its great living tradition, being the account of an American writer's experience in Kyoto, but in another sense it is the cutting edge of an emerging American Zen, which cannot be simply a transplantation of traditional East Asian practices, nor merely a psychological head-trip fashionable in the contemporary scene. It must grow, of itself, from deep down where "The 10,000 things have but a single root." Here is a beginning.

JULY 25, 1978

TAITETSU UNNO
Professor of World Religions
and Chairman, Department of Religion
Smith College

Prologue

An ancient Zen riddle or 'koan' relates that a man hung by his teeth from a pine branch over an abyss. His hands were tied. Exhaustion would soon force him to unclench, and fall free to eternity. But in the meantime a stranger came along the clifftop above his head, bent down, and whispered in his ear the question: 'What is Zen?'

How, or what, to reply?

Scholarship is not enough, and neither is experience, yet one must try. Hence this experiment in journalism which cannot, on the face of it, altogether succeed. Physical experiments at the subatomic level admit a factor of 'indeterminacy' which arises from the experimenter's own involvement. Here the same thing holds true, obviously. The experimenter's own head is a cloud-chamber, where speed-of-light snails streak by, soundlessly court, bump and cavort.

So please bear with me now while I unclench my teeth.

PART ONE *Winter*

He warmeth himself, and saith,
Aha, I am warm!
I have seen the fire.

ISAIAH

Raven

AT SHO-REN-IN, at the darkest season of the year, the giant camphor trees before the gate are green. Yes, even now. Gently, yesterday, they shrugged away the caress of the icy wind. There were three of them, and high up in the shelter of the central one perched a raven. Since ancient times the raven has been seen as an omen of death, especially of death upon the battlefield. Why so? Because the creature is a carrion-eater, clothed in glistening black. All the same, it seemed an omen of good things to come. For you and I too eat the dead in order that the dead may live again in us. Were we to consume living things, the seeds of the spirit, then what?

Within that temple was the God of Judgment, Fudo Myo-o, like anthracite, burned black by the torn almond of flames in which he sat enshrined, and flanked by guardian deities armed with the lotus and the thunderbolt. The lotus blossom, ever unfolding, falling outward without sound or visible motion, conveyed some dim scent of eternity, whereas the thunderbolt appeared quite opposite – the instrument of a moment. Fudo Myo-o, motionless between the two, displayed his sword upright and also let dangle a serpent rope, each knot and vertebra of which appeared to vibrate with burning devils; with ourselves, perhaps?

Unzip your sleeping bag, that placenta of moist darkness in which you live. Crawl out and watch with me now if you can, for you and I are one. So by Saint Patrick and Bodhidharma and our common mother and all who sleep therein I conjure you to remind me . . .

The wilderness past is present, real, here in the belly still, like embers in a cemetery, the still-glowing embers of burnt-out marrow bones. 'Before I formed thee in the belly, I knew thee.'

Absence

A man named Gautama – or Sakyamuni, as the Japanese know him – sat down to meditate in the shade of a bo tree. It was no pioneering effort, technically, for Sakyamuni's ancestors had practised yoga disciplines of meditation for century after century. However, he had passed through terrible austerities which purified his heart and his temper too. He silently vowed not to stir from the spot until enlightenment – or *satori*, as the Japanese call it – was vouchsafed to him. Sakyamuni had resolved to sink, spiritually, into the nowhere, the one-dimensional emptiness at which point all else becomes perfectly clear.

Hours went by while he sat there. Time is a traveller, and this world an inn. Earth turned, day became night, and once again dawn approached India. He had seemed entirely still but now for the first time Sakyamuni stirred and, glancing up, perceived the morning star. That was the only thing needful; that did it; he received enlightenment. His legs must have been numb, by then, from sitting in the so-called lotus position. He stretched them out, no doubt, until their blood-circulation returned to normal. Then after a while he got up to walk back and forth, naked, alone, and blissful.

To actually experience *satori* is the greatest blessing life can bestow. Sakyamuni knew this now. He was to spend the remainder of his life spreading this one message in every way possible. So the great sutras or gospels of the Buddhist religion tell. They leave one crucial question unanswered, however. What did Sakyamuni experience there under the bo tree? What, precisely, was his *satori*? And did it really emanate from the star, or from the heart of Sakyamuni?

His own final word on the subject proved to be no word. He held a flower, silently, and nothing more. This so-called

Flower Sermon, which Sakyamuni delivered upon Vulture Peak when he felt death approaching him, has since become the central mystery and fulcrum of Zen. What did the gesture signify? There is no use looking to Sakyamuni for reply. He has been supplanted by an ideal, impassive, unattainable avatar: the Buddha of religion, who sits with half-closed eyes . . .

Last night I strolled along the Kamo with Walter Gardini the Catholic theologian, and Nishitani the Zen philosopher. The biggest bouncelight known to man, the moon which always comes back strong, irradiated the entire scene: and yet it was nowhere about. Keiji Nishitani, stopping on the path, craned his neck to observe each quarter of the cloudless sky in turn. Then, scratching his bald head in bewilderment he asked, 'Can either of you gentlemen see the moon?'

Eloquently, being from Milan, Gardini stirred the silver-sparkling air with his forefinger: 'No, Sensei, I cannot see the moon!'

I said nothing, being slow.

Courteously, Nishitani giggled. In the reverse-on-purpose manners of conservative Kyoto, this meant that he had something serious to impart. 'In such a case', he said at last, 'you should keep studying Zen until you do.'

After that, we three stood silent for a time, eyeing the refulgent sky and the glittering river – wrinkled children that we were – carved of white jade, all one material.

Daito

Sakyamuni's enlightenment is said to have occurred near the dawn of a December the eighth – a kind of Christmas for Buddhists. Christ came to die for us. The Buddha, on the contrary, came to be born again and show the way to spiritual re-birth. So pious Buddhists celebrate by meditating in the lotus position, like Sakyamuni, from midnight until dawn of the holy day. Such meditation, *zazen*, is the central, non-active practice of Zen-Buddhism in particular. Contemplative Christianity centres upon a comparable non-action: prayer. In a few Zen centres such as the one which I have attended most often during the past year, however, *zazen* discipline alternates with free discussion. This too has been practised for a long time. Daito, the fourteenth-century founder of Daitokuji temple here at Kyoto, was one who not only asked difficult questions but also encouraged his monks to do the same thing in return . . .

The time, between midnight and dawn at Daito's temple, on the eighth of December, long ago. A dozen shaven-headed, black-robed monks, together with their master Daito, sit motion-less on a wooden platform, under the stars. It is intensely cold. By deep slow breathing and concentration, however, each per-son there builds up considerable body-heat, radiating from the belly. Some sweat and shiver both at once. Their ankles, knees, and spines, meanwhile, ache and grow numb, and ache again. At last Daito unclasps his hands and rings a little bell. The monks all bow to him, and then gingerly stretch their limbs. They will be permitted to sit at ease for a few minutes now, and to speak if they like. Daito in turn bows. He has been sitting with one leg stretched out awkwardly in front of him, for he is lame. Now he joins his fingers beneath the withered thigh and shifts his lame leg a little, like a log of wood. A monk breaks the silence:

'Tell us, master. When Sakyamuni saw the star, what did he see?'

'Clean blank nothing,' Daito replies at once.

'But if a person has only so much as just one little speck of dust in his eyes, he may look at a blank and see all sorts of imaginary flowers. Am I right about this, or not?'

Gaze deep and long into the bright night of a flower, not expecting to see anything in particular, and you may find enlightenment there. Any one flower excels the entire universe in splendour and immediacy the moment one regards that flower as it were in God, emanating alone out of the boundless ground of all being whatsoever. The morning star gleams through the flower's empty, fragrant heart, but only when you do not look for it. To seek is not to see; you must really observe creatively.

'My eye is God's eye.' That is to say, true vision answers to something pre-existent in myself.

Zen-Buddhists, here in Kyoto, agree with this. Develop self-power, they suggest, remembering that enlightenment springs from within. Pure-Land Buddhists, however, disagree, and they possess more clout in Japan than does the Zen contingent. They scorn self-power and self-awareness too. Better, they say, to lose yourself in prayer. Other-power is the important thing. Without divine grace, as Christians put it, no true vision.

How about now-power? When you and the flower and *satori* are one, what is there to dissect or apportion? Besides, as a practical matter, timing proves all-important to enlightenment; the moment must be right. But this is not something that can be stalked or snared; consciousness is too coarse-grained to capture or contain so elusive a rightness, such split-second aptness, as this. So the rule is to train and train, like an athlete or a musician, or a dancer for example, until timing becomes an instinctive part of meditation for you. Eventually, you forget time, you forget your surroundings while still being alert to them, you even forget yourself, the pain you may be feeling, and the fact that you continue to breathe. When that happens, even so the chances are that nothing further will occur for you. Still, at that point you may be said to perform a creditable imitation of Sakyamuni under the bo tree. What came to him could come to you, conceivably, providing you conceive it not. Because, although you must be poised to receive *satori*, expectancy is fatal.

Back home in Sussex, England, over the past few years, the birds used to sing while I dug the garden or the children played; only to cease, on a sudden, when one of us paused to listen. Meditation is like that. No wonder, then, that most *satori* comes by seeming chance, 'by accident' as the blind would have it!

Meanwhile, I appear to have lost the thread. Daito and his monks were talking, remember? One of the monks mentioned imaginary flowers, and that sent me haring off after flowers myself. Daito had asserted, sharply and definitely, that Sakyamuni's enlightenment was a complete, clean and perfect blank. The

13

monk in effect responded with the thought that after all Sakyamuni was only human. For human beings, the whole fullness of
emptiness remains and always must remain invisible. Why so?
Because the dust of the world we see obscures it, for one thing.
But even more blinding is fantasy for us. We live in a dream-
world, unconscious and conscious as well, a continual dither of
imaginings. So, what did Daito have to say to that?

'Yes,' the master rejoins without hesitation, 'you are right.
On the mountains tonight, December snow is piling up under
the winds of spring. There are stars also, but no Sakyamuni here!
Whose enlightenment are we talking about?'

The monk has no reply to Daito's question. Soon the bell
rings again, and everyone resumes *zazen*. The thoughts of each
person seem to bubble up ever more slowly, like zeros in the
cold night:

'Birth and death are one and the same . . . Time only seems
to be passing . . . There is no Sakyamuni . . .'

Shinyodo

The Shinyodo bell is a huge bronze gong, tongueless, made to
shout and hum by means of a heavy rope-slung bell-beam like a
battering ram. On New Year's Eve, the local people gather to
awaken the gong's great voice a hundred and eight times, hand-
running, as a means of driving away 'the hundred and eight evil
passions of the dying year'.

Last night the moment came around again. I stood in line
and took my turn at ringing the bell. The man just ahead of
me, a drunken student radical, meanwhile shouted obscenities
in various foreign languages, being frustrated by the fact that
Japanese itself is a deeply polite and almost miraculously clean
tongue. He also wanted to fight, but could hardly keep his feet.
I asked him what the hundred and eight evil passions might be,
specifically, but he gave no coherent reply. Sake wine, bonfire
smoke, sparks flying upward and stars glittering down, had
evidently driven one and all from his mind . . .

A blizzard sheeted dark Manhattan. I was down at the old Stuyvesant Casino, rapt in the rough black spell of Bunk Johnson's music, dancing with a yellow-haired girl. Things happened fast in those days and before the band blared its last Muskrat Ramble down the floor the girl and I were sure we were in love. We walked uptown to her place through the flowing blowing snow, arrived around two in the morning and immediately tumbled into bed. The silence seemed infinite. Manhattan slept, for once, in its immense white eiderdown. We made love like a clenched fist of exhaustion, flesh firmly locked in flesh, and almost motionless, our dancing done for that evening, determined all the same to see whatever it was we thought we might be doing right through to the end and climax if it killed us both . . . But suddenly I was alone. The girl, the bed, the room, the snowbound island of iron and stone all vanished as if taken away in the hand of a whirlwind. Calm, brilliant morning replaced the dark of night. I stood upon a high slope cloaked in sun and snow, beside a wind-bent pine tree. A temple nestled in the grove below, and further down some travellers crossed a humpbacked bridge of red planking. A green river flowed foaming underneath the bridge. Beyond, it plunged into the dark blue ocean, and I wanted to see more of that; I shinnied up the pine tree. The bark was wet and slippery, yet rough enough so I could get a grip on it, staining my fingers red. The horizon rose as I climbed. The rosy branches and the green pine-needles appeared to form eye-sockets, through which I glimpsed new wonders all the time. But now the insides of my thighs were icy from the climb. Clasping the topmost bough, I straightened, straining to see right out over the ocean rim – and then the bough gave way. Falling, I hugged the frigid trunk. My cock crowed with ecstasy. Down I plummeted, through a snowdrift deep into oblivion.

The bed was cold when I woke up. The girl to whom it belonged had gone to work. Mother-naked as I was then, I opened what I thought might be the bathroom door and stepped right out onto the brownstone stoop of the house. I had walked out through the front door, and now it swung shut behind me. Spring lock. Morning had come. It was nice that the snow had stopped. Already some early riser down the street was trying to shovel out his car. 'Aren't you cold, Bud?' he called. I looked down at myself, bumpy and blue, standing up to the shins in drifted snow, and knowing that I would return to Japan eventually, as now.

Covenants

On New Year's Day the mountains to the north kept clapping snowcaps down over their ears and then whipping them off again. The heights were all hidden by swirling storms. In the foreground of my view, meanwhile, the rooftops gleamed sunnily, silver and blue, like swimming fish. Between the distant storms and them a rainbow gleamed, not for a few minutes, nor for an hour, but from early morning until late afternoon. It moved continually, a living creature it seemed to be – pivoting, slowly advancing, flattening out and arching up again, fading and coming back strong, doubling and slimming down, hovering nearby to caress the rooftops with coloured sleeves and, distant once more, featherdusting the quicksilver sky.

A miracle? Of course, but is not all nature miraculous?

Last night, along the low green and brown bank of the wide river, soldiers thronged, thousands of them, tens of thousands, marching as if on air, waving their rifles wildly about and actually leaping for joy. They shouted in triumph, too, although I heard nothing at all, for they had won. The Americans had conquered at last, and now everyone could go home. In my delight at this, I clapped my hands. The sound was thunderous in my own ears. The troops scattered, scurrying like leaves in a whirlwind, as I sat up awake in the dawn light.

What was it, who had placed me there beside the Mekong or the Jordan or the Styx and made me bear brief witness to the ignorant, happy dead? The happy, ignorant dead are many, as Dante said: 'I had not known death had undone so many!'

The armies of the dead infinitely outnumber fleshly battalions, yes. Aside from that, what difference between us? The same river, opposite shores . . .

'Show me where you stand at this very moment!' Masao Abe insists on this. Naturally, I cannot do it. Then he suggests I might as well sit still. It is a steely suggestion of the gentlest kind. Abe puts things in the right order. Although Zen-Buddhist through and through, he begins with the human predicament, not religious rules. And although we meet ritually in a temple, Abe's group scatters at the end of day.

In Japan, ever since the Meiji Restoration, Buddhist temples have been administered by hereditary priests. This is madness, Keiji Nishitani points out. No man is actually born a priest, in the first place, and anyhow a temple ought to be a place of re-birth rather than inheritance. Where there is no seed, nothing grows; hence Buddhist temples hereabouts are apt to be spiritually barren centres for sightseeing, entertainment, and tinsel ritual, with everyone in some sort of costume. Bare-headed, bare-backed, bare-handed, bare-foot Man has no home in the temples now; no place to bare his heart as well. So Nishitani opens his classroom and conducts seminars wherein teachers and students are children together, such as the seminar on the Diamond Sutra which Professor Gardini attends with me.

Social and political problems are peripheral only, Walter Gardini believes. Christian and Buddhist must join hands, not to create an alliance but to enter the central dilemma, Man himself, and deal with that creatively.

Abe, Nishitani and Gardini have been my three chief instructors of late. Dedication to one and the same cause over-rides their intellectual differences, which are great. All three agree that there can be no earthly use in defending the institutions to which they belong. Because, in those institutions *per se*, nothing worth defence is left. Each of these passionately religious men proposes to venture forth from the fortifications of dogma and dogmatics, which are all burnt out in any case, and address themselves to such poor hungry ghosts as myself.

The Diamond Sutra has its own vanishing point, call it begining or ending, to which each separate argument hurtles headlong. *Apratisthita* is the Sanskrit word for this, meaning the unsupported, not-abiding, everything-and-nothing. There, in that one-dimensioned mote of dust – or in that lacquer-black vastitude as the case may appear – one may come to experience Buddha-nature and be free. Such is the promise implicit in the text itself. Meanwhile, however, the text allows not one grass-blade nor inch of ground on which to rest your foot, nor any covering above either; its whole question and answer pattern is designed to strip and even in a sense to stultify the mind. The Diamond Sutra resembles a black and white magpie, a bird of immortality, proudly perched in the midst of an abyss of contradictions avidly collected by itself. Preening its glisten-lettered wings, the magpie screams that from its yellow beak has come the most perfect enlightenment of the Buddhas, together with the Buddhas in person! What can be done with such a claim?

Gardini gave one reply in class the other day. The Diamond Sutra, he suggested, bespeaks the same spiritual reality signified by Saint Paul's pure exultant cry: 'Not I but Christ in me!'

Professor Nishitani was not shocked, as more doctrinaire Buddhists would have been. He gave a birdlike little nod, and then added a few mysterious comments of his own: 'Immediate experience is not such; hence, immediate experience is such. Selflessness is not being selfless; it is a selfless mode of being. First, find purity. Afterwards, be profane in a new way. Finally, be neither one in the old way. Then you are Buddha. Yet do not let Buddha-hood seize you from within. Go free by returning to free others.'

Saviours, buddhas, bodhisatvas, crusaders, reformers, movers and shakers of a saintly kind, how many there have been, and how many are working in the world right now! They have their work cut out for them, plenty to do; sometimes their hearts are cut out too.

Koans

When Bodhidharma, the First Patriarch of Zen, came up from the south into China, the Emperor Wu sent for him and asked some question concerning the highest good. He expected a sermon in reply, but Bodhidharma's answer was:

'Emptiness, and nothing holy.'

Astonished and possibly shocked by that abrupt rejoinder, the Emperor next inquired who Bodhidharma thought he was, to talk so. Bodhidharma frowned, scratched himself, and confessed:

'I do not know.'

Cool, disappointed, Wu dismissed his guest. The Imperial audience was over for that day. Later on, however, when he had given himself an opportunity to ponder what was said, Wu came to feel that Bodhidharma was no fool. He sent for the missionary again, to no avail. The Emperor's emissaries searched far and wide, returning to report that Bodhidharma had disappeared. So poor old Wu died cooler and even more disappointed than before. The south wind however, as a Chinese commentator noted in the margin of this legend, still continued to blow.

The breeze blows where it chooses, they say, and when you do *zazen* your thoughts keep on bubbling up as usual. The point is not to pursue them. You simply sit still and watch, as it were, dimly, not seeing much in the mind's eye. It is as if intellectual bubbles formed in the warm darkness of your gut, swirled slowly up, popped, and dissolved in nothingness. The process does not resemble the 'free-association' techniques developed for psychoanalysis, because it calls for no association of ideas at all, free or not free. You let thought go, and go, without pursuit, until it passes out beyond the borders of your conscious rule, and is gone like Bodhidharma from the Emperor's court.

What Bodhidharma had chosen, in preference to court life and Wu's queries, was to hole up in a cave for nine years, staring at stone. That cave was his soul's womb, and he felt happy there. But finally a would-be disciple found him and managed – by sacrificing an arm, no less – to break in on Bodhidharma's profound meditation. This time, however, the First Patriarch himself was the one to ask questions.

'What do you want?' he began.

'Peace of mind!' was the would-be disciple's reply.

'Show me your mind, in that case, and I'll pacify it.'

'I . . . can't find it now.'

'You see? Already pacified!'

Unlike Bodhidharma's abortive interview with Emperor Wu, this one ended happily. The one-armed would-be disciple who had failed to locate his mind on demand became the Second Patriarch of Zen.

What does the legend mean? Simply that when you no longer seek, but are, then you put the worst of thirsty craving behind, and achieve peace of mind. Fair enough, but all the same you cannot altogether overcome greedy passion while in the flesh. Desire is the entire circuitry of life on this planet. You may refine your appetites no end, but you never in this world so much as begin to eliminate the subtle and all-pervasive pain of being human. Is death an answer, then?

I recently had a dream in which Bodhidharma appeared. He was a floating huddle of a man, rotund, ghostly, with bulging eyes and bulbous brow. Was he grinning, or grimacing? His coarse bristling whiskers made this impossible to tell. 'You seem to be a grown-up man,' he whispered through the beard, 'yet you've never killed anyone. How come?'

'There is a special transmission of Zen outside killing!' I tried to say. But, even as I spoke, a growing sense of doubt brought me awake.

Badly shaken by the dream, I none the less pursued my standard practice of starting the day with *zazen* meditation. To my horror, the same Bodhidharma figure which I had encountered in dream came gliding between the wall and my waking eyes. Fortunately, my instructors had warned that I might occasionally be disturbed by *makyo*, visions of a suspicious nature, while practising *zazen*. I had been told simply to ignore such apparitions. And so, religiously, if that is the word, I stared right through Bodhidharma's image until it frayed out upon the air and disappeared.

Was that really the right thing to do? I was badly frightened for a moment or two, and afterwards less so, which indicates that the answer is yes. In retrospect, however, I would give a good deal to be able to question the figure. What did he mean about killing?

Death is no alien force, nor even a refuge, according to Buddhist philosophy. The Diamond Sutra is just one of the many sacred texts to maintain that no one person has a 'self' to save. No, nor anything other than self to avoid or achieve. Death is the same as birth. The Sixth and final Zen Patriarch – Hui Neng was his name – experienced both death and re-birth at one and the same instant, when he happened to overhear the chanting of the Diamond Sutra.

Yet the words themselves had meant nothing to him, Hui Neng insisted ever afterwards, explaining that all doctrine is by nature dark. Even *zazen* can be a trap, he taught; it is best to pursue no discipline at all. Habit deadens. As for sacred texts, they ought to be destroyed, he said. 'Hui Neng Tearing up the Sutras' was to become a favourite subject of Zen art, later on. Doubtless the old man would have torn up the pictures too, if he could.

One of Hui Neng's many rivals once wrote a poem, a pretty little poem to maintain an old Buddhist doctrine: namely, that the human body itself resembles the bo tree beneath which the Buddha received enlightenment, that the human mind resembles a silvered mirror, and finally that both body and mind ought to be kept dust-free. Hui Neng responded to the poem with a brief, obscure and at the same time brutal blast. There is no bo tree, there is no mirror, there is nothing to dust, he objected. Soon after that exchange occurred, the priest and poet who had been Hui Neng's rival pursued him, begging for enlightenment. Hui Neng obliged with an impossible demand:

'At this very moment, without thinking of good or evil, show me the face you had before your parents were born!'

That was the first of some 1,700 so-called koans – meaning icy conundrums and mad commands – which now constitute the specifically Zen corpus of religious literature and instruction. Hui Neng really started something. Roshis, or Zen masters of the Rinzai sect in particular, set koan after koan to the monks in their charge. Each koan, like Hui Neng's own, appears designed to send disciples so far round the bend that they may meet themselves on the return journey. Examples are:

'Listen to the sound of one hand clapping.'

'Stop the ship on the distant ocean.'

'Tell me, what is one?'

Famous replies to these koans, and hundreds more like them, are common property. Yet these prove small help to the student, for he is required to respond from heart, spontaneously, in such a manner as to convince the roshi that he really does *kushu* or understand the koan to the point of living it. Therefore *sanzen*, as koan-work is known, almost invariably calls for oft-repeated confrontations with one's roshi, leading to ever deeper despair, near-breakdown and – on occasion – breakthrough as well. More than one breakthrough is demanded, as a rule. Just how many, depends upon the novice's own ambition and strength of will rather than his intelligence. Roshi-trainees themselves are said to pass an average 600 koans before receiving permission to set up shop – or rather, temple – as practising roshis themselves. In this respect, Zen ethics recall the old code of psychoanalysis, according to which professionals in that field must themselves have been psychoanalyzed. All but the founder, Freud, that is to say.

Murder

Is there not something brave, and foolish too, in the would-be institution of spontaneity? Zen is a priceless treasure, yes, but the Zen church, like all churches whatsoever, has a thankless mission. It means to guard the treasure and to give it out as well, a little at a time, to suitably deserving acolytes. But from the individual's viewpoint it is a paper dragon coiled around the treasure, breathing verbal brimstone and emitting from between its parchment scales a strong odour of burning heretics. Or it is a committee composed of ordinary men wearing impressive masks, who glumly impose numberless prohibitions while calling upon one to feel free. Or, finally, it resembles the ogre monarch of worldwide legend, who deliberately imposes quite impossible tasks upon the suitors of his only daughter, blinded with desire.

'Go and catch a falling star!'

'Yes, sir!'

One must try, anyhow, because in fact that falling star is the treasure, not the girl. Moreover, the treasure is not really to be given out piecemeal. It is just one thing, long or short, great or small, whether pearl or planet, meteor or match-flame.

'Tell me, what is one?'

A friend who is fairly brilliant and moreover well disciplined in religion – for fifteen years a Benedictine monk – spent no less than eighteen months wrestling with that particular koan. He dreamed up hundreds of replies to the riddle, all of which his roshi rejected with contempt. Then finally my friend suffered an actual dream, a nightmare, wherein the roshi put a knife to his throat, demanding that he either destroy himself or else 'kill somebody back home'. His state of mind at that time was extremely dark and strained. The dream disturbed him so that he determined to act upon it in a way which his roshi would least expect. He would murder the roshi, that was what.

In such a mood, my friend dashed off to his regular morning *sanzen* with the roshi. He found his intended victim deep in meditation. My friend's feet seemed frozen to the tatami-mat, but his clenched fists, his glaring and growling all expressed what was in his heart: a longing to attack and kill.

The roshi, meanwhile, barely glancing up, muttered something in Japanese. 'What am I supposed to do with this idiot?' or words to that effect. Crushed with frustration, my friend rushed out again, into the temple garden. He leaned against a tree, panting for breath, sweating freely, and feeling very foolish now. After a few minutes of this, the roshi showed himself, all smiles, bearing good news. It seemed my friend had finally passed the koan!

A success-story, or not? I felt sufficiently curious to make acquaintance with the roshi in question. A shy cool cat, he seemed, giving sermons with his back to the light, so that it glowed through his prominent ears. Dull sermons, too, forgivably enough. But I was put off by the boast he made, saying 'My eyes are clear', and then quickly turning away. He seemed physically powerful enough to have defended himself against my friend, if the matter had gone that far.

'One is not to be trifled with!' That was my friend's final, albeit wordless, response to the koan. And what makes one not to be trifled with? The fact that one is individual, mutual, and unkillable, all three perhaps, but here words fail. And just because words do fail to convey ultimate truth, slightly dangerous games are made to substitute, in *sanzen*, for discussion.

2:00 a.m.

Walking in mid-air, gingerly I traced the hair-line path of a mandala, half a mile up. Beneath me, clear to the horizon, stretched empty calm blue sea. The mandala was cobweb-thin, and its many right-angle turns hidden from me by the opaqueness of my own body; my feet got in the way. Still and all, I thought I knew where my feet ought to go. But the moment that thought occurred to me, it ceased to apply. I tripped, and now I was falling, slowly down. The blue sea, when I hit, would resist like concrete. I would be killed. At that realization, my body jerked upright, fully awake again. I had dozed off while doing *zazen*!

My heart pounded for a while, sweat streaming down my face, but that was all. I resumed *zazen* and then I was attending a ceremony upon a mountainside. The afternoon was cold, the pines dark green, and the maples crimson. I said no word but set a bowl of blood beneath the trees, a silent offering. It seemed the chill wind in the branches overhead whispered: 'He died into the world!'

So much for my dreaming and so much for *zazen* as well since I seem unable to keep it up for any length of time tonight. Abe-sensei, Song Ryong Hearn, and a few others whom I know could sit all night if necessary, not seeming to move a muscle. Yet they too must be prey to the push-pull of contradictory ideas and emotions which make me so weak and helpless to help myself. They also must feel enlightened at times, and impenetrably stupid as well. To do *zazen* is like laboriously polishing a piece of jade which you can neither see nor feel. Does it even exist, this jade? How can I tell? Without constant polishing, never will it show!

Here is nothing to polish, no jade, nor even a mirror, let alone a mind of my own. Thoughts at random, a shadowy mood, and solitude are all I can claim. I am like anyone and everyone, in the middle of the night alone, although more serious than some. It is no virtue.

Sex, death, dreaming, childhood memories, are the things nobody grasps, nobody understands, and nobody evades for long. The prophets of the so-called higher religions, however, long since hurled the ancient four-horned altars down. Then came the prophets of science, in modern times, to make sexual relations 'safe', delay the falling mace of death, pin dreams like butterflies, and chop off childhood at school. Science accomplished all that as it were in spite, having failed to lay a hand upon the mysteries involved.

The great religions pitch their appeals to dry throat-clearing curiosity and bifocal vision. 'Is there a God, and can we get to heaven?' – that kind of thing. Natural human concern with mysteries closer to home is sick, surely. Call it *angst*, estrangement, alienation. Alienation fits me like a glove . . .

'I shall be with you, even unto the end.' That was Jesus Christ's promise. 'My God, my God, why hast thou forsaken me?' That was his final cry upon the Cross.

Either statement in itself makes a good koan for Christians.

Taken together, they are almost guaranteed to hurl devout persons into a state of intellectual vertigo. How many Catholic priests or Protestant ministers are there who actually *kushu* these mysteries? The New Testament is a document heady with hope, and also red and black with raging rhinoceros doubt. Did Jesus himself suffer abandonment, or did a mere fleshly reminder of the incarnated deity go out with that final despairing shout?

At Tara, at the High King's court, in Ireland, the Druid establishment tossed a hard and sudden koan at Saint Patrick. At this moment, before the King, tell us, they demanded, what is the nature of your Holy Trinity. Explain how your God can be One, and simultaneously Three! The saint passed that koan in a moment. Maintaining a noble silence before his priestly interlocutors, Patrick stooped and plucked a common clover – a three-leaved shamrock – from the ground.

Sakyamuni's own Flower Sermon on Vulture Peak was delivered again by Patrick, who knew it not. Perhaps there really is just one religion, which only saints and bodhisatvas seem to grasp. They all say different things, true, but whoever attempts to speak a universal truth has halfway lost it anyhow.

'Knowing the perfectness and equanimity of things, while they discuss I am silent, and go bathe and admire myself.' The First Patriarch of American poetry, Walt Whitman, said something to that effect. As for Sakyamuni, he bobs balloon-like and benign above the bleak landscape of Buddhist metaphysic – silent as the moon.

Joshu

'Do dogs have souls?'

Children the world over keep wondering about this; and inquiring of their parents, their peers, and their pets as well. They get no satisfactory answer, however. Someone put the same question in slightly different terms to a Zenroshi named Joshu, back in the ninth century. 'Does a dog have Buddha-nature?' was the wry query which a monk tossed at Joshu.

Wu! Joshu responded. The word means no, or nothing, in Chinese. The Japanese pronounce it *Mu*, and they have made Joshu's answer the first and foremost koan used in Rinzai Zen training. In context, what meant *Mu*? Upon that little expletive, all down the centuries, millions of devotees have cracked their skulls.

Buddhist doctrine holds that all sentient beings are in fact Buddhas, if they but knew it, and that every being in existence, right down through plant life to the earth and rocks beneath, is basically sentient. Each and every creature, dogs included, is an aspect of the Buddha-nature, or Buddha-mind, in brief, so an affirmative answer to the monk's query might have appeared appropriate. But it would have been a dull response even though correct. Why treat the canine race as a special case? For the sake of argument? But argument is a bore. Joshu felt that, doubtless. In any case, he wasted no time logic-chopping but instead chopped off the monk's own head with a single word-stroke. His brief bark of a *Wu!* or *Mu!* was unanswerable because it pointed straight at the Buddha-nature or Buddha-mind itself, which is traditionally defined as *sunyata* or nothingness. That much even I understand, but then comes the real koan-work, the purpose of the exercise: to *kushu* nothingness.

A good way to wake up from a bad dream is to squeeze your eyes tight shut *inside* the dream. That seems to open your actual eyes, for some reason. Concentrating on *sunyata* could produce the same effect, conceivably, if only one possessed sufficient faith, sufficient doubt, and sufficient tenacity. Lacking all three, I am an eyeball in a dry skull.

Still, I don't accept the orthodox interpretation of the *Mu* koan. Samurai-style Zen, as it developed in Japan, superimposed the image of a keen word-swordsman upon Joshu. Yet Chinese tradition holds that he was a gentle person who never once struck or shouted at the pilgrims who came to him, and who survived on this planet for no less than a hundred and twenty years. That hardly jibes with the Japanese view that Joshu was a fiend for 'dharma-combat', on tiptoe to decapitate tricky questioners in debate. Chances are, then, that he replied to the monk's question straight from the heart, in all humility. How?

Not with a bow-wow, not with a grr, not with a woof either, but with an inscrutably Pekinese *Wu!* Or *Mu!* in Japanese.

Compassion calls for taking fellow-creatures into one's heart, from which they may then speak, and Joshu was compassionate. Saint Francis of Assisi preached to the birds. Joshu spoke for the dogs, among other creatures. His response to the question did mean nothing, yes, but everything as well, just like the sounds that come from canine throats. Animals speak the word of God wholeheartedly. For them it is not paradoxical, but direct.

In the daytime, that window over there gives an overview of a tin rooftop belonging to a neighbour's cat. She likes dozing in the open air, or sitting up to gaze down on the passing show. Her name I do not know; but the school children hereabouts address her from a distance as 'Miaou!' – and she replies in kind, while keeping well out of their way. Sometimes she will acknowledge my presence in the window at her back by giving me a slow across-the-shoulder look and a whisker-twitch of comment. In her aloof and feline fashion she accepts me, but is that surprising? Why?

There was a time when I felt reasonably at home in the world . . .

Yesterday, the north wind rattled my windowpane and Miaou showed herself in a sudden finger of sunshine. The sky darkened soon again, but she appeared reluctant to go back inside. She was waiting for something, what could it be? I made coffee. While I was doing so, a big brown tomcat bounded up out of nowhere to assault my friend. The pot boiled over.

Before I reached the window again, the tom was gone. Licking her bites and mewing pitifully, my friend writhed where she lay, until a spate of cold rain forced her back indoors. Spring seemed on the way; after an hour or so, sunshine returned, and so did Miaou. She looked contented now, nourishing something new, I guessed, inside herself . . .

Joshu, who was a friend to animals, took lessons at the feet of an abrupt abbot named Nansen. The east and west wings of Nansen's monastery both claimed the same cat for a mascot. Eventually, they begged the abbot to adjudicate their dispute. Nansen's response was surprising, to say the least. Seizing the poor object of their envious concern by the neck he flourished a cleaver over it and shouted:

'Quick, somebody, say the right word!'

Nansen's pedagogical purpose seems plain enough in retrospect. The abbot was roundly challenging his monks to overcome dualistic thinking in the case of the cat. Far from being a special mascot of the east wing or the west wing, or even of the monastery as a whole, that cat belonged to nobody and nothing except itself. Like all living creatures, it was an integrated being, a Buddha in its own right.

The Judgment of Solomon, as related in the Bible, made a similar point. Two women came before the King, both claiming to be mothers of one and the same infant. Let it be cut in half, then, Solomon ruled, and one half given to each woman! Upon hearing this judgment, one claimant smiled complacently. The other claimant, however, screamed out: 'I am not the mother, and I have no rights here, but let my baby live!' Solomon thereupon signalled to the executioner. The infant, still alive and well, was given to the woman who had withdrawn her claim. 'Whoever its mother may be,' Solomon told her, 'you are the mother.' The King possessed an understanding heart. So did abbot Nansen, no doubt.

However, nobody could think of what to say. The cleaver descended. The cat fell away in two exceedingly bloody pieces. Not a pretty story.

Joshu had been out working in the fields all day. On his return, as he was removing his clogs to step indoors, someone told him about Nansen's summary judgment. Joshu stooped down without a word, retrieved his muddy clogs and set them both on top of his head. Barefoot, alone, he stumbled off into the darkening fields again.

When that strange behaviour was reported to Nansen, the abbot sighed: 'If only Joshu had been around earlier!'

We must have dualistic thinking, just as we require two feet in order to walk. But at a higher level, so to speak, dualism gives way to direct intuition of the truth. Joshu demonstrated that by putting the clogs on his head, but why did he then depart?

His fellow-monks' unwillingness to recognize the cat's Buddha-nature was nothing new from Joshu's point of view. What was new was that Nansen had presumed to reveal in blood the breathing wholeness of the cat's existence, precisely by slashing it in two. This must have come as a terrific shock, for Joshu himself could never look upon any fellow-creature as a mere object of abstract debate or proto-scientific experiment. He may have been the only man in the whole monastery, however, to actually feel compassion for the cat that was. If so, the realization would have been crushing to Joshu, and Nansen his teacher no more.

East-West

Huntington Cairns, the secret sage of Washington, D.C., once took me out to Rock Creek Park to view the Adams Memorial. Henry Adams had commissioned the statue from Homer St. Gaudens, he explained. Its purpose was to convey a great ideal which – Adams claimed – 'any Chinese coolie would understand.' What ideal? Both Adams and the sculptor kept it to themselves. Cairns had previously invited a Chinese Ambassador to view the memorial, in hopes that that personage might provide some clue, but the Ambassador seemed as baffled as everyone else.

To me, the life-size bronze appeared pawky, resembling a substitute football player, a wide end warming the bench in the rain on a Saturday afternoon – with a soggy blanket drawn up over his head – who knows full well the game is lost and that in any case he himself will not be called upon to play. Cairns smiled, Buddha-like, at my irreverent critique. The secret ideal, he said, had recently been laid bare. A letter from Adams to

St. Gaudens, unpublished before, gave the whole game away. What did the letter call for?

I could not guess. That evening, Cairns put the same question to a mutual friend – a girl with a Taoist background – and showed her a photo of the statue. 'The intellectual acceptance of the inevitable,' was her response. Cairns turned pale as she spoke, for Henry Adams had employed the very same words. Adams' hidden purpose, moreover, had been to smuggle that 'Eastern ideal' into a Western centre of power.

Such half-tangible traffic runs the other way as well. Consider for instance the green bronze nude sitting stoop-backed upon a boulder, and taut with cogitation, his muscles like paralyzed mice beneath the skin, who dominates the entrance court of Kyoto's National Museum. Ask a Taoist philosopher or Buddhist intellectual what Rodin's immortal *Thinker* seems to be doing there, and you invite the part-wistful, part-contemptuous reply: 'Pursuing illusion!' For the deliberately intense and self-cramping posture of the figure suggests that some very hard hunt must be going on inside his head. Images of the Buddha typically demonstrate an opposite process. Sitting erect, straight-backed, with a small blissful smile, the Buddha of Asiatic art appears content to let his thoughts go, to let them bud, blossom and fall like flowers, endlessly. To ask what passes through Buddha's mind would be like asking about the weather.

Rodin, however, was not concerned with nature; let alone the universal harmony which, in Taoism at least, nature reflects. This artist pointed always to Man. His *Thinker* has problems, obviously, like me. Perhaps the figure emerged from a solitary dip in a lake only to find his clothes stolen away and gone in the meantime. He does not know quite what to do about it, for in his environment being naked implies some helplessness and even absurdity. Yet the figure seems vaguely heroic as well. He might be Odysseus naked on the beach, following his final shipwreck. Or, Adam after the Fall! Consciousness West, in short.

Doing *zazen* helps me to iron out that kind of consciousness for a brief spell, following which I invariably revert to brow-creased, wrinkle-brained ratiocination. That suits me too. Apparently I am neither a true Westerner nor yet again consistently Eastern. Is anyone?

Wings

A woman wearing ordinary leatherette bedroom slippers stood in a running brook of the garden at Heian-ji, yesterday noon. She wore a white bandana as a face-mask. She was busily sweeping the stream with a broom, shoving the silvery water hard along its pebble bed. As I watched, it seemed that I had been a dragon once. Grinning from ear to ear, I stretched my claws to seize the moon; and, having that, reeled all up and down the sky in joy. I stood on the horizon, then; I swallowed the moon like an aspirin. Immediately, I fell into the sea. A small naked eel I was now, exploring eagerly until I found the river mouth of home. Upstream I swam, swallowing everything I found, until the hook was in my throat.

'Lady of the stream,' my heart cried out, 'please sweep me back into the sky once more!'

Where did that happen? Where occurred the part that was not physical, not at Heian-ji? It is impossible to say. In Tokyo, while giving a lecture the other day, I wrote down four categories of consciousness on the blackboard. First, things really understood from personal experience. Second, things gathered by inference or deduction. Third, things guessed at or theorized about. Fourth and finally, things intuited or imagined. I felt rather pleased with that quaternity, until a young Japanese at the back of the hall came to his feet with an easy motion to demand: 'How about physical things, are they excluded?'

Of course not, I said. Consciousness works all of a piece, and is a single field fraught with physical energies.

'In that case,' he rejoined at once, 'your diagram becomes a big blur, it all blends together, doesn't it?' And he was right. His insight equalled mine; he stole one of my eyes and cut my own perceiving powers right in half on the spot, sad to relate. Someone whose insight surpasses, rather than equalling my own, would be a better student for my purposes . . .

The New England Transcendentalists Ralph Waldo Emerson and Henry David Thoreau must have been equals, more or less, in spiritual vision. Like one-eyed men who had bumped heads together dully, each on his blind side, they complained of each other in their respective journals.

Thoreau was much given to what he called 'reverie', and would sit in his sunny doorway at Walden Pond, quite still, for hours and hours at a time. His habit must have been very like *zazen*. The birds doubtless made themselves free of his heart, not of his house only. Even the distant highway seems to have become part of his nerve-ends at last, for he would return to himself at the pinch of cartwheels upon the road. Forgetting time as he sat still, Thoreau spread himself out in space, invisibly, to become a human map or miles-wide psychic skin, or finally just an open circle.

Ouroborus, the Snake Who Swallows His Own Tail, was the ancient Greek symbol for timelessness. Or rather, for spacetime *cum* eternity. Logic chops the snake in half and speaks of time over against the eternal. However, they seem to be one and the same creature. Zeno saw that and demonstrated it by means of a *regressus in infinitum*, namely the mathematical fable of the race between swift-footed Achilles and the tortoise – in which the tortoise proves to be victorious. Spacetime and eternity are objective and subjective aspects of something far beyond human ken, which must reconcile them. Hence 'The last will be first' after all, and the best way to break all prisons may be simply sitting still – as in *zazen*.

Invited to join an experiment in communal living at Brook Farm, Emerson ruefully declined. He had not conquered his own house, he explained. To raise the siege of that hencoop, as Emerson called it, and 'march away to a pretended siege of Babylon', would have been irresponsible from his viewpoint. As for me, I keep moving around. Before I was able to wander in reality, I did so in imagination as a regular thing. For the past fifteen years or more, I have been a family-style vagabond. Afraid to grow up, am I, like Peter Pan? Certainly no Emerson.

As on Peter Pan's magic island, children occasionally look about themselves and conclude that there are no grown-ups, only pirates, with perhaps a sprinkling of grey-haired kids. Well-meaning adults try to capture such observant little beings and insist they join the pirate crew. But they, the children, may decide, as I did early on, that one's best course lies far beyond the brown delta waters and the jungle steam, and the dry acid fumes of the dark city, far out across clean seas before the wings of imagination fray.

Well, anyhow, I went that way. Now the time for stillness has come.

Those meetings for *zazen* practice at Myoshinji have already helped me more than I realized at first. On giving them up for a while I found I missed the little bell, so musical, the fragrance of incense, the clear chill air drifting in around the paper screens from the garden, and finally the thin dry clack of the wooden clapper shattering me to wakefulness again. I missed the mutual tolerance of some thirty fellow-novices all doing more or less the same things together in close company, and even the dim vision of Abe-sensei's bare feet crossing the tatami-mat before my half-closed eyes, as he silently made the rounds with his disciplinary *keisaku*, his whacking-stick, poised.

Everyone there suffered, no doubt of it. Pain is an essential factor in the learning process. Pain, plus group support, plus unassertive yet relentless moral pressure from the top, teach one, little by little how to practise *zazen*. Yet paradoxically enough my very first effort met with a miraculous moment of blessing, such as would not occur again for a long time . . .

It happened thanks to a kitten, which scampered into the *zendo* and romped about at will while all of us sat very still. It was not difficult to guess what was happening, from the sounds the kitten made, but of course nobody dared turn to look. Closer to me came the kitten, scurrying, circling, pausing, and then making a long jump or two, stalking motes of dust, perhaps, in the slices of sunlight which slanted between the screens. At last the kitten reached the very tatami-mat upon which I kept my eyes fixed, and there it paused, with raised forepaw, swivelling its neat blunt head around to gaze at me. As it did so, the creature's eyes widened. Who or what did it recognize? Settling back in an expectant crouch, it searched my face with pale astonished eyes. Did it expect some little bird to pop out of my nose, or what? Motionless, questioning, the kitten seemed to mirror my own posture. I felt that I could glimpse myself through its eyes, and that the reverse might also be true. The kitten was inside my thought somewhere, not just out there, and I was part of its intense awareness now as well – both of us motionless under the same soundless bell of crystal, like thoughts paired, mirroring each other, in a single mind.

The 'Western' meditation which I used to practise involved thinking about something, circling it intellectually, closing in to embrace and finally trying to interpenetrate the object of my thought. *Zazen* meditation, however, is not like that. It has to do with emptiness, the void, which might be signified by alertness and rest at the same time. Breathing, too, plays into this kind of emptiness – which is in fact full of renewal – both inside and out. No thought is called for. Rather, I sometimes repeat a mantrum, a sacred sound-pattern of some sort, meaningless or not, to still the mind. Or, I may find myself sighing, or even purring for example, as part of the ordinary breathing process. No harm in that, but who is it that produces the sound? Indeed, who breathes? What breathes? If anyone asked me such a question while I was engaged in doing *zazen*, I would not know what to tell him.

Still, the practice can be agonizing to my back and legs. Worse yet, it does sometimes result in rather frightening chest-pains. To ease the pains I walk a lot. One morning recently I reached a little bridge over the Kamo river, and paused there to enjoy the brave glitter of seagulls upon the ice-veiled reaches of fresh water. What were they doing so far inland? Eating garbage, mainly. They were refugees, I suppose, from the great

Mitsubishi oil spill which has polluted the nearest shores. I stood a while, wearily wondering about ourselves. What is our present food, our condition, and where do we humans belong? No answers came. The clash of crystallized ideas, the clatter of shattered opinions continuously tumbling downstairs, the harsh and brittle music of intellect at war with itself – all this is no longer for me, in any case. I wish to dance to a differing drum. Namely the heart, whether it hurts or leaps for joy as the case may be. One hand clapping, in short.

Song Ryong

'When I was a child, I thought as a child,' Saint Paul says, and that sounds reasonable; but in fact it is not true for me or for any other human being. No, when I was a child then I saw 'face to face'. Now, right now is the time when I can only glimpse things 'through a glass, darkly'. Turn up the light of reason, and the glass immediately darkens; vision dims. That's how it really is.

Once long ago a pilgrim found himself in the desert beyond Tibet. It was a starless night, the sky like black lacquer, the dusty wind importunately pulling at his hair and beard, and the jagged rocks rising to wound his stumbling feet. The pilgrim had hoped to reach a great spiritual teacher, beyond the wilderness, but now that hope was gone. He might well die of thirst before morning. Fervently, the pilgrim prayed to Amida Buddha – the Lord of Light – for help. Immediately, his foot struck something that was not a stone. It was a silver bowl filled to the brim with pure cold melting snow. The pilgrim drank all he could, in his weakened condition, and then, with a cracked prayer of gratitude, sank down upon the sand. He fell asleep.

When dawn awakened him, the pilgrim reached once again for the saving silver bowl. It proved to be a human skull. Bits of flesh, fringing the bare bone still, showed that the skull must have been full of life until quite recently. Besides, the hollow of it held what seemed to be brain-fluid, swimming thick with maggots like dirty grey thoughts. The pilgrim vomited at the sight. As he did so, *satori* came to him. He turned homeward, without delay. That which he sought was accomplished. He had found his teacher, and his temple as well – the temple of the skull.

The Reverend Song Ryong Hearn related that story, back in Los Angeles, the day I told him I meant to study Zen in Japan. I was still unsure whether Zen-Buddhism should be imported to America. 'Poison mushrooms,' I called it then.

Song Ryong's story should have been a sufficient reply. In his compassion, however, he went on to say: 'Sakyamuni shot an arrow into the air. It passed across the high mountains from India to China, then Korea, and on across salt water to Japan. But why should the arrow stop there? Poisoned or not, it is already across the Pacific, and across the American mountains and plains, nor will it stop there either.'

'Oh, my America, my New Found Land!' was John Donne's exultant cry. Death and sex, alternately, were much on that poet's mind. The American wilderness he wrote about had nothing to do with geography, needless to say. It was the penetrable and yet endless mystery which he discovered anew each time his best girl undressed. But modern urban America could never be an image for sexual love, only for sexual relations at their most negative, fuelled by fiercely greedy self-assertion, sweat-glazed, heavy all the way. America is crabbed after two centuries, a dowager with iron filings in her pores. Ego-land, united we stand, cursed with bitter complaint and self-complacent bullying. Yet saintly characters thrive in such surroundings too. Song Ryong Hearn, for example.

Zazen keeps him strong; Song Ryong sits like a stone. 'People dread *zazen* like a desert trip,' he told me once. 'It seems to be dead, dry, empty. But if they sit long enough and dig deep enough they find everything is all right after all. There is water in the desert.'

That much at least I too have learned, here in Japan. Doing *zazen*, you keep your eyes open. You recognize yourself and the world around, and then as time goes by you become dimly conscious of some third factor which is neither you nor it, but which seems to embrace, energize, dissolve and ultimately reconstitute what went before. It is not pleasant, as a rule, nor unpleasant either. But calming and strengthening, yes. Sometimes it resembles a passing summer cloud which cools and darkens the whole landscape for a while, so that everything remains familiar yet seems new-born in the welcome shadow.

Arrows

Once they had made the world, the fabricating deities planned a picnic to celebrate their work. First, they spread a living tablecloth out on the grass. That was Chaos. From its cool white sparkle they drew music, meat, and wine at will. Chaos produced out of its own bodiless and passive being whatever they might ask. 'How very helpful!' cried the deities, and they decided to reward Chaos with the most precious gift in their possession. Namely, Self-awareness. So each one grasped a corner of the tablecloth, and pulled. Chaos came apart with a sigh, vanishing from between the deities' fingers. Where it had been spread out, the grass lay dry and dead. The feast of the gods ended in confusion . . .

John Godolphin Bennett used to call upon his many disciples, and on me as well, to try and create a double-pointed arrow of awareness. It ought to point to whatever you were doing, and to yourself at the same time, so John explained. He drew the concept from his own master, Gurdjieff. I did not like it. The two points of such an arrow would be sex and intellect, it seemed to me, elements better left a little dull. I spoke for keeping straight the hollow shaft between the two . . . but all that seems needlessly esoteric now. Gurdjieff was certainly a very brilliant man, highly charged sexually, and John displayed much the same pattern in his turn. The other night, to my astonishment, he dropped by for a visit –

'I had to be tough on my disciples,' he remarked. 'They needed plenty of shocks. Not you, however – I considered you my friend. With you I could relax and take it easy, or ignore your presence as the case might be. Which reminds me, I must fly out again tonight.'

He clutched his shrivelled barrel-chest exploringly. His fingers were chalk-white, beautifully formed, and still strong-looking. 'Yes,' he decided, in a voice already faint, 'I've got my ticket,' and with those words he vanished away.

Was that my dream, or his? To put the question differently, just where on earth did it take place? For John is dead, and I have been the one to ignore him of late. Now, let me remember our best day together for his sake:

The once and future King Arthur of Camelot reigned from a hill near Glastonbury, according to John. His own summer home was in that area, he explained on the phone, inviting me and my family down for the week-end. He would be happy to reveal to us Arthur's erstwhile court. Naturally, we went. My children were just the right age for such an adventure, and so were his own two youngest ones. John himself was already in his mid-seventies by then, but very strong. He spear-headed the expedition up the steep slope, which was encrusted with briars. Being in shorts, he suffered hundreds of scratches thereby. Mosquitoes and voracious blackflies slavered round his straining legs, his arms, and craggy, happy face. Scrambling over fallen trees and leaping mucky ditches one after another, we soon became convinced that we were on the right track – a trackless one, at that. Such an impregnable site must actually be Camelot, and no wonder it had been overlooked until now! By the time we emerged on the flat pastureland which crowned the hill, we were all exhausted, except John, and yet glowing with the excitement of the thing. To penetrate history in this way seemed to us a beautiful, inestimable boon. But what was that herd of cows, with a few bulls among them, spread out along the crest? Were they mild reincarnations of Arthur's knights and ladies, perhaps? How had these incurious animals come up, I asked myself – by helicopter? Darkly they moved, their horns lifting and lowering again in the light of the setting sun. I did not see how we could possibly descend the hill again before nightfall.

'Oh, that's no problem,' and John pointed out a gate at the far side of the pasture. 'There's a cowpath down, just a half-hour walk.'

'Couldn't we have come up that way?' one of his children asked aloud. The question had immediately occurred to all hands; only the youngest member of the expedition dared put it into words.

'I guess so,' John told her, straight-faced. 'In that case, would we have arrived here?'

Zen, as practised in Japan, would have appealed to John Bennett; the martial arts especially. Unlike myself, he would have leaped to learn what he could of *kendo* swordsmanship, and doubtless practised archery. There is a double-arrow of awareness in that too. Zen archers stand meditating in a sense on their targets, with drawn bows, until everything seems right, and only then let fly as it were by the way.

A friend of my youth practised the art here at Kyoto, until he actually reached the point of snuffing out a candle flame with an arrow shot from fifty feet away. Incredulous at his own success, he rushed the length of the temple hall to recover his arrow and see if it bore a scorch-mark. For which breach of decorum, then and there, the abbot dismissed him.

At Sanju-Sangendo, recently, I witnessed the great archery contest of the year. It was beautiful to watch, but those fellows kept missing the bull's eye, and I could not understand why. Their best efforts were pathetic compared with the marksmanship displayed by an old priest behind the doors of the temple. Kneeling on a platform above the milling crowd and manipulating a delicate pair of tongs in a vase filled with ice-cold water, the priest rapidly flipped single flashing drops onto the heads of every visitor who passed beneath.

Whether it descend as diamonds in cross-section, or salt for psychological wounds perhaps, the snow could not care less upon whom it settles. So it was with this benediction from above. The priest was impartial. Dip, flick, plip, pauseless, he bent to his work. The eye of the bull, where is it? I came away feeling refreshed by one drop of water. There seemed more life in that one drop than in whole Sutras I have studied.

The Sutras often resemble the telephone poles to which I pressed my ears in childhood, dimly humming. That must be why the legendary sage Gutei kept silence all the way, and answered every question by pointing one finger. When death approached at last, he pointed heavenward, joking perhaps.

Yamabushi

The Japanese word *Setsubun* stands for the Feast of the Joint in the Bamboo. Last week at Shogo-in, a chorus of old women celebrated *Setsubun* by chanting the Diamond Sutra. The small silver bells suspended from their blue-veined hands made an icy sound, reminding me of the poet Sengai's curious *haiku*:

'The wind blows out the candle; the Diamond collapses into ash.'

Figures wrapped up to the eyes in white were moving through the throng which filled the temple yard. They carried willow branches to which were attached one-line poems for sale. Meanwhile a young sentinel on the porch of the temple sprang up from his kneeling posture, sweepingly unsheathed his sword, and made an urgent slash in the thin freezing air. No one paid the slightest attention. Expressionless, he cleaned his blade, sheathed it, and sank to his knees again – awaiting further trouble.

In a courtyard off to one side a bonfire sparkled, built of large tree-roots. A *yamabushi* or mountain priest, a big heavy-set man, firm on his feet, tended the fire. I stepped close to it, stretching my hands out to catch the fire's warmth. The *yama-bushi* was neither welcoming nor the reverse. We stood opposite each other, we two alone, across the fire, for twenty minutes or more. His soft white boots, slit at the toe, resembled hoofs. Expertly, he would nudge a tree-root with one foot, every now and then, keeping the fire bright. The *yamabushi* wore loose cotton garments lightly dyed with saffron, and over them a body-harness hung with large purple pompoms like a circus clown's. His face was smooth, strong-featured, and adorned with a sparse brown goatee. His age must have been about fifty. A tiny black top-hat tied with string perched precariously upon the *yamabushi's* brow. His entire costume had a comic air, in short, as he himself did not. In fact the man reminded me of a traditional Noh drama wherein a similarly accoutred character accosted a small, stoical orphan boy named Ushiwaka.

The boy's position appeared hopeless, for he was of the recently crushed Minamoto clan. In time, however, this boy was to exact full vengeance for his father's death and destroy the conquering Heike family. Now, the drama's first act consisted of nothing but a conversation between Ushiwaka and the kindly *yamabushi*, for Noh is notoriously short on plot. In the second and final act, however, the *yamabushi* came back again in his true form. He was really the *Tengu* or Goblin Monarch of Mount Kurama. This time he wore a purple top-hat like a puff of smoke atop his thick red mane. His visage was maroon-coloured and cleaver-sharp. His wide purple sleeves were silver-laced for easy soaring; his orange trousers glittered as he danced. An owl-feather fan well served the *Tengu* for a sword, as he demonstrated various tricks of combat for the boy. Astral, awesome, unstable as a bird upon the wind, he glided, swooped, and stamped his foot. Pale, motionless, Ushiwaka observed the *Tengu* carefully, then advanced upon him with a sudden motion to seize his trailing sleeve. Well pleased by this, the Goblin Monarch vanished across an airy bridge, and the boy followed him. End of play. Not much to it, except that Ushiwaka was every boy in the wistful end-of-childhood year or two preceding puberty. A *Tengu* of some kind dances for every boy about that time, helping him to prepare for the fire-pimpled warfare and hair-tent bivouacs of adolescence . . .

Next day, I passed by Shogo-in again, to find that some two hundred priests from the mountains, all caparisoned like my silent friend of the bonfire, had foregathered there. They formed a hollow square, seated around a structure of logs and evergreen

42

branches. Obviously, an important ceremony was soon to begin, and so I joined the growing crowd of spectators to watch the priestly assembly attack the structure with words, arrows, a sword, a halberd and finally a forked stick. After that, they set fire to it. Yellow smoke billowed in the bitter wind. A huge drum boomed. The assembled shamans began loudly chanting and rhythmically rolling their prayer-beads between their palms. Some of their number meanwhile ritually burned thousands of sticks inscribed with names. Hot ashes rained down on all heads. The participants were coughing and wheezing now, flaying with handkerchiefs at the cinders which scorched their necks. All except one, that is to say. Namely, the man whose fire I had shared.

Remorselessly, the magic rite went on and on, lasting for some hours altogether. Surely the cinders must have seared the skin of my particular acquaintance, and the smoke must have stifled him too at times, yet he gave no sign of distress but sat alert and seemingly content throughout.

Afterwards, at the temple gate, I lingered on to watch the departing procession of clown-costumed priests – my man among the rest. On the way out, he paused as if looking around for someone, and then caught my eye. Deliberately, with a faint, ironic smile, he bowed to me. Feeling impressed and baffled both at once, I reverently returned his bow. His blood-shot eyes gleamed as if to say, 'We have a karmic connection, you and I.' Then he passed briskly on through the gate and away.

Men of the mountains, latter-day shamans, are such priests as he. When they climb the high slopes, they chant as they go up, a single phrase, conducive of purification of the heart. Such men surely know, even better than practitioners of Zen, the significance of the ancient saying:

'First it is a mountain; then it isn't; then it is!'

Who really sent me up Mount Hiei, soon after *Setsubun*, and who designed the spell which fell upon me afterwards? Can it have been that same shaman?

Shaggy, hump-shouldered Mount Hiei looms north-east of

Kyoto; it guards the city in the direction from which evil influences are believed to come. No less than a thousand temples, inhabited by a large army of warrior-monks, used to exist upon its slopes. The mountain bristled like a hedgehog with sacred pagodas, in feudal times. Far from protecting Kyoto, however, the monks of Mount Hiei would often terrorize the city. So the grim Shogun Nobunaga finally ringed the whole mountain with fire, burned out the temples and slaughtered every monk therein.

Red-faced, red-bottomed, blue-eyed monkeys inhabit Hiei today. Unseemly beasts they may be, but not bloodthirsty as their predecessors were. There is a turnpike to the top of the mountain which hums and grinds with heavy tourist traffic, and where temples once nestled on the pine-clad slopes are posh resort hotels.

I went up by bus with the rest. On that climb, no purification. Near the crest were monkeys begging food, people eating, *pachinko* pinball games, coin-operated telescopes, snack and souvenir shops, pine woods, and snow. Below me, Kyoto appeared bedridden, sheeted in smog. Eastwards, Lake Biwa displayed its ashen pollution from shore to shore. Above my head a few large birds appeared to skate, stiff-winged, upon the thin ice of the upper atmosphere. From their vantage points, I suppose Mount Hiei resembled a dragon sadly hacked about and scotched where it crouched, foul of breath, broken by the toll-road-builders' bulldozers and the huge cement snowshoes of concessionaires. Did those birds nest within the dragon's chewed-off ears, or where? Ah, space is great, I thought. Man cannot pollute all of that, for it includes sun, moon and stars.

The all-encompassing Void which is celebrated in Buddhist religion seemed greater still just then, an idea wherein the cosmos appears but one of a billion spinning bubbles! But thoughts are all collapsible. The Void could also be a misty chasm, soul-pool, or plastic-button factory, ready to swallow me down without a qualm!

Such was the first hint of the nightmare which overtook me

shortly before dawn of the following day. In my dream I attempted to climb Hiei on foot, but the mountain kept falling inside-out. The more I shouted for help in my struggle to stand upright, the greater the deathly silence of the slope. The closer I approached the snowy peak, the further I fell down into a sheer granite funnel. The harder I scrambled, the more desperately I clutched and clung, the less there was to grasp in any direction. Worse than all this, however, was my awakening. Because, when I opened my eyes wide to the darkness of pre-dawn, the nightmare still continued as before. Sitting up in bed, I assumed the *zazen* posture and tried to call upon Amida Buddha's protection – to no avail. I knew that I was certifiably insane at that moment, and there was not one thing I could do about it, but that hardly mattered. What did matter was the pain, the agony of illusion tearing me up the middle, and through the midst of which I twisted and tore in turn, like a steadily deepening wound.

Saint Patrick of Ireland suffered an extremely severe ordeal on the night following a Druid ritual in which he had refused to partake. The ceremony culminated, as Patrick's own story relates, in a feast of honey, a food which the Druids held sacred to the sun. Patrick permitted not one drop of honey to pass his own lips, for he feared it. Then in the night, as he put the case, Satan fell upon him like a great boulder, so that he could not stir hand or foot but lay quite still under the weight that was on him, all through the night until the sun arose. As it came up through the trees, Patrick saw the sun, and then he shouted 'Helios!' Thereupon he was released; Satan departed. Patrick was himself again. But why, the Saint asked later on, had he called upon the sun – in Greek, strangely enough – to lighten the desperate dark strait in which he found himself? Latin was familiar to him, but not Greek, so why did he not call upon Sol, rather than Helios, to split and cast aside the great invisible boulder which was pressing him down into the earth at that time?

The words which came to me to cry out were in English: 'Let the mountain be!'

That saved me. Sanity returned, for reasons I can never

know. I cannot know because the interface between bliss and madness is thin as the skin of an eyeball.

Call

Since I am human my pillow is Jacob's pillow. Being human, I too wrestle with what I cannot understand, both waking and sleeping. Being human, I am part of Israel to come. Because not just the Hebrew but the whole human race is the chosen one. Chosen for sacrifice, at least. I do not know what more. When I am practising *zazen*, however, and the nerve-structure of my left hip and thigh begins behaving like a closed circuit of pain-signals, it reminds me of Patriarch Jacob and how his hip was wrenched in dream. A little pain well underlines the little one can know.

Hence the use of *keisaku*, the long thin back-whacking stick, in most group practice of *zazen*. Abe-sensei employs this ritual instrument only on request, such being the rule of the society which he keeps together, but all the same every sitting at Myoshinji is punctuated by the terrible whistle and crack of the *keisaku* and, though nobody so much as glances up to see who has been hit, everyone feels the blow fall across his own shoulder-blades. Moreover, it makes each person in the *zendo* sit straighter, for a while, than before. The enterprise in which one and all are engaged is hopeless, useless on the face of it, yet serious if nothing else, so the *keisaku* reminds me. Not crime and punishment, nor even error and correction, but simple sitting and hitting, in reverence and innocence as well, characterizes Zen practice. It seems absurd, and yet . . .

I was tired this morning when I began *zazen*. But soon, as so often happens, something occurred to give me energy and encouragement. My rather blurred gaze was resting on a patch of sunlight. Softly, out of the blue, a bird-shadow brushed across the patch and coolly caressed my brow as well. I sat astonished, when the same thing happened over again in reverse, going the other way. A pigeon, most likely, had winged its way up to the roof outside, perched for a moment and then drifted down again – in perfect silence, that was the strange thing.

In Oriental calligraphy, the brush-strokes imitate bird-shadows, do they not? Alan Priest was the man who first pointed that out to me. He had a special fondness for light-hearted art, and liked seeing birds fly. But Priest intensely disliked having visitors disturb the empty quietude of the Far Eastern Wing at the Metropolitan Museum in New York, where he presided as Curator. He kept the place dark, hoping that nobody would show up. However, the gloom of the place appealed to me, and since I lived nearby at the time I used to drop in there a good deal. Priest therefore, to get rid of me, instructed his guards to snap the lights on full whenever I turned up. Although I did not know him yet, that seemed a personal affront. I stalked into his private office to protest. There Priest immediately disarmed me with a warm welcome, and then proceeded to show me all sorts of treasures not on public view. Since I was ignorant, and enjoying the things at hand, I spoke hardly at all. That seemed to please the old curmudgeon. In the course of time he befriended me . . .

Cigarettes suspended like tusks from the corners of his lips, the smoke from them encircling his ears, a martini in each pink fist, and dragon-laughter bubbling from within – so that crazy old philosopher returns to mind. On the single occasion when he received me in his rooms opposite the Museum, however, Priest was uncharacteristically dignified. He served green tea that afternoon, a sacred beverage in Zen-Buddhism.

'How does one become a Zen master?' I asked him, innocently enough.

Leaning suddenly across the tea things, Priest clapped me on the knee. Then he settled back comfortably, looked me straight in the eye and said, 'Like that!'

Astonished and at a loss for words, I spread my hands.

'It's done,' Priest said. 'In young manhood, in China, I myself received the Wordless Transmission. I was empowered to pass it on, and this I have now done. You are a Zen master too, and there is nothing you can do about it now!'

Was I dreaming, or what? To make sure, I actually pinched myself. Priest soberly observed that boyish action.

'Well, I don't feel any different, thank God,' I said.

'You will, though,' Priest serenely rejoined.

He was absolutely sincere; no doubt of it, but was he right? Ever since that long-ago afternoon, I must admit, I have been drawn to Zen. But I have not come any distance at all; this too I know. And in the meantime Priest himself has passed on. His ashes lie here in Kyoto.

Why have I failed? It has not been for lack of opportunity. Enlightening moments seem to shower down around the shadow that I am, without relieving its obscurity. Authoritative instructors in Zen and other religions have welcomed me and tried their best to acquaint me with true doctrine as they see it. But I am an ungrateful sort, suspicious of Gospel-stocked or Sutra-stocked intellects. I keep asking personal questions because the spirit seems to me a personal thing – a thing no better acquainted with institutions than birds are with buildings. Birds may nest under the eaves of a house, and spirit may inhabit a church office too but not intrinsically. My questions have not been deep enough, or sympathetic enough. Result, disappointment all round. Sometimes the Zen establishment looks to me like a whitewashed hippopotamus, with a few present-day saints and sages gleaming like the odd tooth in the old hippo's friendly gaping jaws. Meanwhile I have suffered for my unwillingness to accept the protection which religious institutions extend.

I go reeling around the great nowhere-going highway of the world, and feel put-upon when the faceless drivers of heavy, fast-moving vehicles loom up and crowd me into the ditch. But what am I? A goose-pimpled crazy on a skewed glass bicycle, continually crashing into scribbled walls . . .

Machines and battleship-grey men command the world, it seems, and yet I have been blessed and blessed again. My failure is my own. *Ban butsu do kon*, I tell myself, 'The 10,000 things have but one root.' Yet I do not bend my thoughts in its direction.

Lacking self-discipline, I do not even begin to dig deep enough to come upon the 'one root'. Twisted, forked, rough-textured, buried deep beneath the heart, in darkness hard to penetrate, that root must grow straight down and down. Well, go to sleep . . .

It is raining, rain on the windowpane, sweet sound of spring coming. These beautiful dim raindrops fall nowhere else!

The apparition of these faces in the
   crowd;
Petals on a wet, black bough.

EZRA POUND

Visions

SOME PEOPLE can see through things at times. Occluded realms
become as it were transparent to them. But I have not the power;
I am relatively dull and thick. Yet, by way of compensation perhaps, something like the reverse does happen in my case. Instead
of my seeing through to the invisible, the invisible pops out at
me. Sometimes it takes hallucinatory form. This morning, for
instance, when I opened my eyes and stared at the red towel
which I had used to cover the mirror near the foot of my bed –

Darkly burning, buzzing, like brazen bumblebee wings, the
vision was at first, breaking the china-blue non-thought in
which I lay. Then it solidified to shape a human head, which
leaned half-upright on a hard pillow or possibly a chopping-
block. It is universally noticed, and yet very odd all the same,
that apparitions tend to come equipped with elaborate costumes
and props. This one had its pillow, on which to rest, but no body
at all. It was red in colour, and a couple of feet in height. Its thin
lips curved widely downwards, drooling spittle. Its small slant
eyes were muddy with concentrated malevolence. Meaning
what? I was too upset to question it. Instead, I closed my eyes
hard, and when I opened them again the vision was already
dissolving, melting down into red cloth.

Lust and rage, I know about. Sometimes they seem to be
heavy chains. But the Sixth Patriarch, Hui Neng, said that too is
an illusion. The passions in themselves, Hui Neng declared, 'are
nothing but enlightenment.' Perhaps the apparition which came
to me might have demonstrated something of that sort, if only I
had been a little calmer and more patient . . .

In his eagerness to perceive the sublunary realm allotted to him, primal Man tore away the planetary covering and leaned gently down. Nature, gazing up, met the glance of his male eye and his female eye, and felt his shadow upon her, and was neuter no longer but alive with love. Primal man meanwhile saw her as well, stretched out in his own reflection in the water below, and much desired to join with her, to live in her for a while. For him, desire and action were one and the same thing. Thus, instantaneously, he came to occupy a form devoid of reason. Nature, having received him whom she loved, folded him to herself, and so they were united.

Man has ever since slept in the finite, in Nature's arms, dreamily stirring every now and then, it may be, but not even beginning to awaken again because he feels no intrinsic desire to return to the infinite – at least not yet. We children of primal Man and Nature, however, do sometimes burn with just such a yearning; albeit for what we never knew. We are natural and supernatural both at once, to our distress. A heavenly hermaphrodite was our father; yet we find ourselves split into pairs and sexually magnetized to join forces as best we can, one with another. Unsleeping and self-nourishing Nature gave us birth, yet we find ourselves subject to the strong bonds of sleep and the sharp goads of hunger and thirst. All this because our actual first parents set such precedents in their passionate strange way of 'sleeping together' from the primal dawn until the present moment and beyond. For we belong to them; we children are their dream, and yet sometimes it appears that the Son of Man has nowhere to lay his head.

Valentines

Two people fall in love; a momentous occasion, why? Easy to say it must be momentous because their whole future lives are at stake, but they themselves could not care less about that part. *Now* is the time for lovers. They do not care whether dawn ever comes. Who needs yet another day? If only this one night would last forever, they say, meaning it.

The evening before last, there was a terrific downpour. When it let up a little, I thought of strolling in the Gosho, the Imperial Palace Park. No one would be about, I supposed. A walk in the cool drizzle would clear my head perhaps, and help me to sleep later on. But I got a surprise instead, which left me cloudier than before. My path curved close beneath a tree and there, in its shelter, a pair of lovers coupled on the ground. I nearly stumbled on them, in the shadows, but not quite. Pausing hardly a moment in my embarrassment I raised my umbrella as a gesture of salute, and hurried on.

In their intensity, those two must have been soaked straight through. Could they be taking pleasure in each other so uncomfortably as that? Yes of course, they were being what they were; lovers, so let it storm. Lovers, and who did that foreigner, that strange person wandering along under his umbrella, who did he think he was?

The same, the same, although alone. That encounter coloured my heart valentine red in the rain, as it still does tonight.

Lovers are those who have nothing and everything to lose, let go. Because, whether or not their heads may recognize the fact, their hearts know that love at its most intense will cut across and lean right through a man, and through a woman, looking for something else, looking beyond. So lovers run the risk of being outstripped by their own passion, although the love that looks beyond is rare enough. It seems a commonplace, but no, for it is overwhelming, unsupportable. The fascination of the thing, however, is common – universal, to tell the truth. Infrequently met with in life are love and death. In human imagination, however, they reign; there love is queen, and death her consort . . .

Question: Which came first, the chicken or the egg?

Answer: You did.

Question: In that case, which are you?

Answer: *Sokutaku no ki.*

Question: Who he?

Soku is Japanese for the special sound made by a mother hen tapping at an egg with her beak, to help the chick inside hatch out. *Taku* is the sound the chick itself makes tapping from within. As for *no ki*, that signifies nothing but timing. So a patient roshi explained to me.

He was talking about *satori*, was he not? The poet William Blake meant much the same thing when he said that in every day there is a moment which the devil cannot find. The devil can find it very well in fact, unless you get there first.

When I first opened Blake, at age sixteen or thereabouts, he reached out from the book to stick a little question point-first, like a pen-knife, right into the palm of my hand. The words I do not remember. The point, however, was this. How can you tell that a sparrow is not a feathered spark of ecstasy, closed, shut away by your five senses?

But the senses are holy, I protested then, as I still do. The human body is as sacred as the sparrow's own. What would Blake say to that? For weeks, I went around mumbling to myself about it.

Shopping

This robber who dwells in your own house and hates you for the sake of what he himself loves – kill him! This tomb which you carry around on your back – destroy it! The ascetics of ancient Alexandria ranted on like that; so did the Puritan Fathers of New England where I was born. They were wrong to condemn the body, but right to rave against all dull blind wallowing perhaps. Because when you overburden the senses with sensation, when you wilfully overload the electrochemical currents of their own operation, you in effect short-circuit them. In such a case, of course, the senses continue to function, you may well feel more pleasure or more pain than previously, and yet in actuality you can no longer see what you should see nor hear what you should hear . . .

Because she had brushed her hair straight back, and tied it in a ponytail, no one recognized the comedienne. In films, her hair was a polished waterfall of peek-a-boo platinum, half concealing a heart-shaped vulnerable little face. This way, though, she seemed an open secret, invisible to everyone except myself. Closer she came, closer, stepping along by the brassiere counter and pausing not at all. She wore a crisp-starched toreador blouse; the little bobblings of her breasts disturbed its lace. She came on warm inside, yet cool as any matador. I licked my dry lips watching her. Being an actress, she was doubtless conscious of my hot stare. She came straight towards me, unhesitatingly. But I was still too young and shy, not to say cowardly, for someone like her. Turning away, I nipped into the shelter of a porcelain display. That was the end of it, I thought. A moment later, however, she followed me into the cup and saucer castle I had chosen as a hiding-place. I turned to face her, and she gazed frankly up into my eyes. The lacy frill of her toreador costume brushed my shirt-front. She smelled like paradise. Worshipfully, I gaped; and then she winked.

'Of course you could, and I could, boy,' that wink said plain as day. 'We could, you know, and both enjoy, if we had any opportunity!'

With that, she touched her left forefinger to her pink, pink lips, and spun away. Wickedly prim, she pranced off down the stairs into the Cutlery Department. A lion might have bounded after her, but my sign is Taurus – Taurus amid the porcelain. I stood nonplussed, a paralyzed bull in a china-shop. What an actress, and what a perfect comic turn she had staged for herself and me alone! She lived up to her name that time, *Veronica*, the classic pass in Spanish bullfighting . . .

A courtesan once asked Socrates how it was that she had such a bustling business while his friends, on the other hand, were few. 'You cater to a practically universal yearning,' Socrates replied. 'I don't.'

Softly, after long silence, the courtesan said: 'Let me be your friend also, Socrates!'

Ikkyu

Sex, and *satori*. In the whole history of Zen, just one great master overtly linked these natural twins: Ikkyu. An Emperor's natural son, born proud, Ikkyu was perforce apprenticed to a Zen master in early childhood. In youth, he tore loose to become a formidable fish-eater, truculent sake-drinker, and iron brothel customer. In maturity, Ikkyu was a poet and calligrapher of note, a tea-master, and no mean flute player. In old age, having survived most of the locally tumultuous fifteenth century, Ikkyu served as the Chief Abbot of Daitokuji Temple. From the beginning to the end he remained an ardent priest of Zen. It was a tissue of contradictions, a coarse and splendid fabric, but no hair-shirt, that Ikkyu wore and gloried in, flamboyant all the way.

Each and every dawn hour at Daitokuji, to this day, his life-size wooden effigy receives ritual breakfast on a tray. The forty-minute breakfast ceremony never varies in the least – no more so than the miso bean soup, rice, pickles and bitter tea which make up Ikkyu's effigy's menu. Thus is honoured the man who described himself in one poem as –

Hating incense,
Distrusting satori,
Disbelieving talk of Zen,
Thoroughly despising priestly piety,
Wrinkling my nose with disgust here in the dimness of the Buddha Hall.

In his last years Ikkyu became passionately involved with a little singer, a blind girl. The priests at Daitokuji suggest that sexual impotence must have cast a blight upon their idol's last affair. Why so? His poems to the girl are steeped in sadness, they explain. Moreover, undeniably, those same poems do harp on cunnilingus and fellatio. They are in that respect quite explicit, although the tone which pervades each one is mystical at the same time. In my own view, it is not impossible that Ikkyu opted for a sort of sexual tea-ceremony. Because he was flaccid? No. More likely, he chose to avoid fathering a child whom he would soon have to leave fatherless – being old. As to the sadness of the whole affair, last times are not easy. April may be the cruellest month, but September is more melancholy. Moreover, the girl must have badly wanted his child. The greatest liberation is fruitfulness, which she had not experienced. So frustration there must have been, especially for her, as Ikkyu of all people would have understood.

His very last poem, however, had nothing to do with love, nor with anyone but himself. In paraphrase it reads: 'After years and years and years and years of dimly sweating and straining, I excrete my faeces and present the same at Buddha's altar.'

Meaning what? Did the most overtly and reverently sensual of all Zen masters conclude in the end that the body itself is shit? His mind was going too; how about that? Ikkyu's last brief piece of writing appears to be absolutely negative. Or is it absolutely positive? Deliberately, and not without humour either, Ikkyu bequeathes a coarse and concrete image for disciples to empty again if they can. Look, he says in effect, I have digested what I can from both body and mind. Now I drop both in death, giving them back to earth and sky.

Ikkyu's last poem comes as close as can be to the ancient and still urgent Buddhist injunction – stated in the Diamond Sutra and elsewhere – calling upon man to produce a thought which is not supported by anything. He made it finally, I like to think, although his words do not quite incorporate the event. Words never can do so, since they themselves constitute support – or 'attachment'.

'Produce a thought which is nowhere supported, nowhere dwelling, without attachment of any kind.' But detachment, equally, will not do. Detachment, too, loops you back to your own skin-prison, albeit by a circuitous route. Only know that wide secular highways and multitudinous sacred paths or *dharmas* exist, bringing no advancement. Receiving zero, plunge to freedom if you can. Not until Sakyamuni saw that his favourite disciple had gained not one thing graspable from all his teaching, did he then turn and make that man a Buddha too. Such was the first 'wordless transmission' celebrated in Zen, from which the light of emptiness has ever since been said to flow.

Tunnel

There lived a gold-tanned long-legged cheerleader, up in Newton, Mass., and I stole away from boarding-school to see her. An evening in May, adrift with motes of light and darkness mixed, and time turning as it did then – not as on a watch-face but with infinite urgency – I chose for going to the girl. Or did I choose? Anyhow, there I was, turning at the corner to enter the dim green and purple insect-humming quietude of her tree-lined street, making for her house with its wide front porch and low-slung hammock half-obscured by honeysuckle vines. She would be waiting, yet I was slow; thinking of her, naturally, but also of a nightmare which plagued me as a boy. Namely, the one in which I walked through just such gathering darkness as this, knowing that a fierce fiery-bearded troll no more than a foot high would shortly come tap-tapping along behind me – and pass by at a nerve-shattering scurry.

I heard footsteps approaching from behind. Sexual energy is no one's possession, but like an electrically charged hair on loan from some inconceivable parent underground, invisible whisker from a flint-clawed jaguar, and the supernatural is sudden everywhere. I turned to look.

A man approached, alone, bigger than I, ten years older perhaps, having a pale matinee-idol face and black hair snakily tangled across his brow. He moved fast, bent forward, as if some stinging sort of thing were after him. He turned up his coat-collar as he came, for self-protection it seemed. The evening was very mild. I stepped aside to let him pass. Doing so, he glanced once at me, with a black look, both wobbly and powerful. Sincere, that flash expressed the glassy, thin-ice sincerity of those who have little or no self-sense or self-control. Embarrassed, I lowered my eyes. He wore ice-cream-coloured flannel trousers, creased sharp, and two-tone shoes clicking on out ahead; metal tabs on the heels would make that small scrapey racket. The dark trees rustled like a steel-brush riff, and then I knew him: Gene Krupa, the jazz drummer. I had seen him before, on the Ritz Roof in Boston, playing with Benny Goodman's band. He was well in front of me now, nearing my girl's house. Would he stop there? Well, why shouldn't he do so? She was not my girl. I knew that, really. If Krupa snapped his fingers for her, she would gladly oblige him instead of me. Blind rage swept me now, jealousy. Why? No reason; there were no intellectual bones to this feeling. To experience jealousy is like swimming blind smack into a poisonous jellyfish. The clamminess, the strangeness, and the syringe sting, together with the sense that nothing has actually occurred, are similar.

The light above her porch door had been left on, as a signal to whom? It cast Krupa's shadow back and back, almost to my feet. He kept walking. The light swept his shadow, shorter now, into the street and forward once again. His ice-cream pants melted into obscurity.

'Did you see that fellow go by just now? I thought he might be you at first. He was too old, though. I've been saving myself for someone a little younger, you know, like you. Hello, boy. Mom and Dad have gone to the movies tonight. My thought.'

Such was her greeting, sweet and to the point. Clicking off the light, I asked whether she had recognized the person.

'Who? . . .' she began. My tongue stopped her question. Clumsily, I seized present desire in both hands.

She was a tender teacher who soon let me in – at which moment, by a splendid coincidence, the streetlamps automatically clicked on. From her vine-sheltered lair and private darkness on the porch, my just-pierced friend gazed out upon a long transverse tunnel of young illuminated leaves. And so did I; in fact I was the girl and the trembling leaf tunnel too and even the musician who had gone before. I was all things and nothing, in a word, because the moment when the street lit up the emptiness inside me suffered illumination as well. I came as it were from *sunyata*, which is Sanskrit for the blessed void of which the universe itself is built and instantaneously destroyed. In the moment of coming I sank back to be a simple electron droplet of sheer, scratchless joy.

Strippers

Adolescence: A tunnel of moist fires, romantic, and comic, by turns . . .

As I was riding east out of Detroit one night a heavy lady slipped unasked into my pullman berth. Her limbs were strong and thick. She had beer on her breath. Her breasts were small, curiously pear-shaped. For many hundred miles through the night she did astonishments to me. The dawn revealed that she possessed a perfect, middle-aged, Grecian profile.

'Let's talk a while,' I whispered, 'I'm just dead!'

'Don't give me that routine, sonny,' she whispered back, dimpling. 'You're not dead yet, by a long shot. If you were dead, you know, you'd be all cold and lying out there on the aisle floor instead of here with yours truly. Besides, I've never quite killed anyone – not even my husband.'

Lifting her gleaming arms, she switched on the berth-light. Her patent leather purse glared from its nest of soiled nylons in the overhead rack. She reached for it, and plunged her wet hand into its red belly. 'My husband!' she repeated rather anxiously, fishing around inside the purse. Out slid a snapshot, at last, of a circus strongman wearing a lionskin. 'I make more than him,' she said placidly. 'When the circus folds down for the winter, Fred lays around drinking beer. Me, I'm a buyer for a big department store. My trade knows no season. Summer, winter, it's all the same to me. I waste no time. That reminds me of something. Listen, an hour from now Fred will be meeting me in Philadelphia. I've got to go make myself sweet for him, you know? So, bye-bye sweetie. Wait. You must be a student, am I right? Guessed it. You'll never have me to learn you no more. So, what will you do?'

'Sleep!' I informed her. I would be riding on through to New York.

'Okay, but if you're still awake when I get off this train, take a peek through the window.'

I dozed off instantly, but when the train halted at Philadelphia I was jolted awake again. The woman who stepped down to the platform looked bigger than I would have imagined, a pudding of a person and yet neo-classical. Her patent-leather purse and pumps were primly twinkling in the early morning light. The grimy eyes in her heavily powdered face glanced up at my window. She did not smile. Her husband was coming along the platform now, eagerly striding. In his serge suit, the strongman too looked overweight. He said something. The woman turned to meet him and her coat swung open as she spread her arms. Her gloved hands met at the back of his neck ... My dirty window blurred the scene; the train was under way again. Depleted, wistful, nude, and like a ghost whom the approach of sunrise whisks home to the tomb, I sped horizontally on.

The fat department-store buyer and happy lion-skinned cuckold, where are they tonight? For that matter, where is the me she knew? All gone, surely, and yet something remains. There is something, or nothing as the case may be, which changes not. The next time I woke up, the train was plunging in under Park Avenue, New York, and the whole Earth had meanwhile approached somewhat closer to a distant star called Vega which we see as nothing but a diamond point of light ...

'Skin!' The painter Yves Tanguy exclaimed one day, stretching his clever hands in my direction as if to demonstrate a neat but too-tight pair of gloves. 'How I yearn to spring out of my skin and drop the whole thing forever!'

The delicious cocktails he served had made us both expansive. Coarsely, I asked which of his many skins he had in mind, adding the observation that each human being is a regular Chinese nest of skins, from the gut outwards, all derived from the lowly worm.

That brought him up out of his chair. 'Let's walk in the garden,' Tanguy suggested. 'Summer came early to Connecticut this year. I keep telling myself it's lovely here.'

Strolling about with him, I heard a faint pathetic cheeping

sound which rose out of the grass before my feet. I stopped to look. But Tanguy, barely breaking stride, brought his crepe-soled boot neatly down upon the robin-chick. Its little gut protruded from its pleading beak, and popped. 'Too bad,' the painter said. 'I have to do that all the time. I can't locate the nests these things fall from, you see. The trees around here are too tall. So I just squash each chick to sleep.'

The sun was warm; I shivered anyhow, feeling featherless myself, and fallen far indeed, down from the tree of stars.

Ordinary consciousness is a sense like the rest, a sixth sense which coordinates the pre-existing five. And thinking also is too often dull blind wallowing, in facts and opinions for example. Cram consciousness too much; it becomes a rubbish dump of dry-fill material, smelly and smouldering still. Disgust sets in; sleep overcomes at last; that's how it goes. Mind in itself meanwhile abides patiently, as it were the ocean or the sky . . .

I was drunk that night at the Crawford House on Scollay Square when first his left hand rattling like sleet on cymbals and rims alerted me to her existence. A big plain girl she seemed, young and alone under the lights in her g-string, not interesting. Slowly, her pale belly began to suck and roll, while with one foot he built up a heartbeat on the big drum. She twirled her breasts also, tossing sweat from the bruise-coloured nipples, while he stroked magnesium rhythms in about the girl. Now he was thrashing like a sulphur crocodile down a Nile of broken glass. Passionately she clapped her talcumed thighs to echo every fulmination in the flesh, shaking her buttocks as if whipped. . . . Then like limp damask suddenly the drum fell dumb. The room was silent and yet she contorted still, alone with the curling cigar-smoke in her klieglight cone, her wet cheeks aflame now with rage and shame. I saw the drummer in the shadows smirk. To put her on the hook like this had been his little joke. After a tense minute the girl got herself back under control. The black-lidded eyes in her dull face tearfully glimmered; she hid them with her hands. Her shoulders shook. Was she really crying, or was she laughing after all? She ran offstage. The lights came up, and just as they did so the image of Marsyas – flayed – floated for a moment before me.

Marsyas, yes; his best-known legend has to do with a contest in music, waged between himself and Apollo. The satyr played first. Gently pursing his wide lips, and tapping his delicate hoof, he blew a few notes down through his reed pipes. That was all, yet the loud brook paused at Marsyas' feet and stilled itself reflectively. His music delighted the earth, the water, and the sky, and every creature equally. It promised all that freedom, love, the colours of the meadow and the songs of the grove can bestow, including immortality.

Then Apollo, lord of the sun, made a song of how flesh binds mortals in, and praised the gates of skin, and stroked a rainbow from his golden lyre. Dog-eyed, darkened, panting, the satyr shrank down before the god. Already he anticipated martyrdom and, true enough, Apollo had him skinned alive ...

There was once a clever man who had the privilege of living with a saint for a time and yet never felt sure of him. The saint appeared so very simple and empty as to be 'not all there'. Instead of praying, for example, the saint used to talk to himself out loud:

'Are you awake yet?'

'Yes, I am!'

'Try to remain so. Don't be stupid today.'

'I'll try!'

– and so on. It seemed rather pitiable, looking back, especially now that the saint had passed away. So said the saint's erstwhile companion to a friend.

'He's dead, is he?' the friend remarked. 'If you were to call him now, calling out bravely to him just as he did to himself, would he answer?'

The clever fellow made no reply; he was silent, struck dumb by what seemed to him a stupid question.

The saint of that old Zen story may have been a satyr skinned alive, a second Marsyas, one who came through the sacrifice in such a way that he could never die. 'He' being the true naked and nowhere 'I' – not skin and bones, nor even consciousness.

Accept, if you can, the knife that strips you free.

Occult

Jesus on the Cross recognizes that he has omitted something essential from his life; the joys of sexual love are still unknown to him. So, by a supreme effort of will, Jesus survives his ordeal, and returns from the tomb. He greets the Disciples, briefly, and then takes off, not heavenward but to a seaside temple of the Goddess of Love. There he meets a beautiful priestess and . . .

That parable, by D. H. Lawrence, made a profound impression on someone whom I was. 'Whatever the dead may know,' Lawrence concluded, 'they cannot know the joys of being alive in the flesh.' The words come back to me because I often quoted them to unfeeling girls, unwilling priestesses.

An early Christian papyrus, unearthed at Nag Hamadi in upper Egypt, indicates Jesus was no virgin when he died. Paradoxically, the papyrus also implies that all of us are virginal, whatever we may do. Why so? Because the depths of our hearts were and are in existence 'before' us – and will not taste death. This is expressed in a very Zen-like Beatitude which the text attributes to Jesus himself: *Blessed is he who was before he came into being!*

But the notion of Original Purity, said some early Christian Fathers sensibly enough, could be used to excuse any crime under the sun on the grounds that the pure can do no wrong. Let us therefore extirpate the concept if we can! So books such as the Nag Hamadi 'Gospel According to Thomas' were banned, went underground, and largely vanished. Still, the old problem remained: the double nature of the human condition. Religions the world over keep right on speaking to the pure in each individual heart, offering encouragement and reminding each person of his heavenly origin. Then again they keep snapping out a harsh line at the same time: repent, repent, for you have sinned, nor is there any good in you. Some faiths accentuate the positive, others the negative aspects of human nature. But since each human being personally represents the entire spectrum, religions too must generally address all of it. Sects which fail to do so fade away after a time, into sickly-sweet sentiment or dire polemics as the case may be . . .

Elephanta shrine cuts right into the rock of a turtle-shaped island. The statues there are not free-standing but actively rooted in stone. Dim grainy light floats among them like thoughts. Being alone in the cavern once, I circled slowly to its silent core: a polished black granite phallus standing upright in a vulva-like stone socket. There were wildflower offerings, like pubic hair, and ribbons of incense wreathing up. I passed my hands through the incense, intending to touch the stone itself, but no. A living sheath, as it were, shone from the stone, pressing outwards against my fingertips. I could have overcome this palpable resistance and simply thrust my fingers through the illusion or whatever it was. That might have been an intriguing experiment to make, but not in my mood of the moment. Daunted, I cast myself down before the Hindu idol, on my knees, and pressed my forehead to the floor of the cavern.

Then what? Why then, nothing. After a while, I got up again and backed away to the cavern door. Heat and cold contended in the rock-cut exit. The turbid air streamed through my shirt and hair. There was some deathly bitter taint about it. Turning, I plunged on out to the huge light and heat of the sun. I could see some distance now across the bay of Bombay. Something was out there which I did not feel able to believe. Namely a second phallus, silver-gleaming, hundreds of feet high!

It was, I later learned, an atomic reactor which had been donated to India by the United States Government, and which was proving useful for the development of nuclear bombs. As for the shape of the installation, that was just 'a nice touch' on the architect's part – to imitate the ancient Hindu lingams on a giant scale.

Individuals are brought up short, every so often, by some

65

sacred mystery. Governments cannot be. Tasting death with no sensation of distress, they complacently exhale pollution.

A week or two after leaving Elephanta, I found myself standing motionless in the knee-deep water of a rice-paddy. An old ascetic came along the causeway, walking firmly, without haste. His robe was extremely ragged. His long silver beard half concealed the bones of his ribcage. His young eyes glittered in the dusk. He seemed to be following in the footsteps of someone else. I turned to look, and sure enough, an exuberant dwarf was running on ahead along the path. Now the dwarf paused in mid-stride to kick one leg straight up over his head, with fierce and astonishing joy. He danced straight on again, and in a moment he was gone. The ascetic, meanwhile, had stopped upon the path and turned to stare in my direction. His gaze was piercing and yet perfectly impersonal. He did not seem to understand that I saw him as well. I might have been some unfamiliar bird, or fish perhaps, for all the recognition he accorded me. I thought of calling out a greeting of some kind, but just then the bubble of my dream abruptly popped. Once more I lay in the village of Ellora, cocooned in my mosquito-net.

Had that dream-figure observed me disappear? 'You never know', he may have told himself, smoothing his frosty beard with rootlike fingers, 'what strange outlandish men you are going to meet on the path of Vishnu!'

Photog

Once I said to Diane – an early arrow in my heart, she was – that I would like to learn self-hypnosis in order to die painlessly. That did not seem to strike her as a cowardly idea. She had barely passed fourteen, that summer at Cummington. Giving each other back-rubs started our friendship. It was on a sweaty Sunday afternoon, in the long grass back of the cemetery, that I first sensed with my fingertips the snake of light, the delicious serpent, hidden within her spinal cord.

The last time we met, we touched not. Nor did we light so

much as a candle together as the winter gloom of four o'clock in the afternoon descended on her studio room. I reminded her of when she had written with a fountain pen in the palm of my hand.

'What did I write?' she asked, and without pausing for my answer she went on: 'Yes, bone, that was it. I wrote the word because, although you did a lot more talking then, what you said seemed like crying of the bones. I myself was sad for no reason that I could guess. Our bodies must have been unquiet, I suppose.'

Her shadow-pocked face gleamed silver-distant in the dusk, like some small private moon. She remembered well, I thought. Aloud, I said nothing. Her face appeared to waver as she turned, passing from full to hollow and from hollow to full. Watchful, dimly glittering, it kept part of my heart between its lips.

Silently, for I tend to be silent as well as slow, I put a question to Diane.

'I don't think so,' she responded, just as if I had spoken. 'Not childhood, no, there's something else we're looking for, something we're not even aware of yet, although it must be here.'

Whatever the secret may have been, her serpent knew it. Meaning the light-filled snake which I had long since been privileged to stroke through Diane's downy skin. Meaning, again, the creature which so artfully deployed and multiplied itself up and down her developing-tubs, in the form of tender and scarifying black and white photographs.

Diane found painless death at last by slashing her own wrists in a warm bath. The artful serpent dried out of her there, only to reappear months later in the great museums of Venice, London and New York. Three major exhibitions, one right after the other, generated sudden fame for Diane who was dead, and for her shadowy serpent-flickering images of suffering and inchoate desire. For one who loved her, irony of ironies.

Eden is here somewhere, Diane, since long before the Tree of Knowledge came to bloom.

Eats

The Japanese have an amiable custom of designating their foremost artists 'National Treasures'. Can people who are so honoured leave the country without an export permit? When they abuse themselves, is it vandalism? One of their number, a *kabuki* actor, died not long since from eating blowfish – a gourmet dish which he well knew could prove fatal, but he was feeling rebellious – in a Kyoto restaurant. *Art Strikes Back, Masterpiece Runs Amuck*, the headlines might have read. Soon after that event, I went to see another 'National Treasure' dance the role of the little geisha Toshima on the *kabuki* stage. Like all *kabuki* actors the performer was male; moreover he was sixty-eight years old. His name: Utaema. His genius: incredibly acid, sweet, and sinuous at one and the same time. The character he portrayed was just passing her prime, filled with tender misery and nostalgia, stunted at heart, and clever. Utaema set this complex creature in motion, one thought following another, gesture by gesture, as freely as clouds up above or blowfish cavorting in the deep. Behind the mask of Toshima's white-painted face, inside her fragrant flowered kimono, was anybody home? A three-times unreal question, that, yet Utaema gave weight to it so long as the curtain remained up.

I was eating apricot candy meanwhile, and vividly experiencing theatre in the round. An old geisha – Toshima thirty years on – had leaned across with irresistible grace and spirit to put the candy in my hand and see that I popped it into my mouth as well. Sinking back again, she gently waved her arms and fan in time to the music; she evidently knew the dance by heart. To create a character on stage, unforgettably and yet in a truly playful spirit, cannot be easy. But to serve a fellow mortal selflessly, in a similar spirit of play, as the aged geisha had done to me, is possibly more difficult still.

How about meditation, then? Is *zazen* ever so disciplined, so deep, that it becomes pure fun? Utaema's performance was astonishingly brilliant, yes. The old geisha's spontaneous gesture, her little gift to me, had been not brilliant, not astonishing, but simply perfect – which seems better yet. What would perfect meditation call for? Joyously stirring chaos with a jewelled spear.

Or, possibly, sitting under a tree with your mouth open, looking up, waiting for a ripe plum to drop. The Chinese characters for mouth and tree, set vertically with mouth at the bottom, stand for wisdom. The same two characters reversed, with mouth on top, spell starvation and folly, obviously.

'Should I continue to indulge myself by eating meat and drinking wine, or not?' Late in the eighth century, a pilgrim from the Yellow River valley put that query to a Zen sage named Ma Tsu. Seekers often inquire about such things. One must go on eating and drinking, obviously, but what? Not beans, by any means! So thundered the ancient sage of Magna Graecia, Pythagoras. Not demon rum, by gum, says Billy Graham. Not pot, you lot, the cops insist; and so on. Ma Tsu's response was more benign. 'You take real pleasure in meat and wine,' he suggested. Relieved, salivating already, the pilgrim nodded eagerly. 'You might find bliss in their absence,' Ma Tsu added, 'or not.' Thus he gained a promising recruit. Teach self-control to a person of sinful history and strong appetites; sure enough he soon begins seething with energy and reaching, reaching out for genuine joy...

For all their appearance of simple-mindedness, the ancient purification ceremonies performed at Mibudera Temple are infinitely obscure. They take place out of doors, on a deep verandah, to the very slow accompaniment of gong, flute, and drum only. The dancers repeat everything three times or more, and the effect is hypnotic, to say the least. What I saw yesterday began with a solitary person in a rather tensely smiling female mask, bent on purifying the whole stage area. She brought on a goofy, goggle-eyed, black-faced exorcist to help with this, then dismissed him again. After a time, she subsided into meditation. Thereupon a horrendously huge devil danced in, awakened the woman from her trance and chased her into the wings. He had the stage to himself now. What would he do? Why, play, naturally, but how? Would he play fair, for example?

Dark and crimson, mixed, was this devil, his armpits steaming and his great hands thatched with hair. To disguise himself would not be easy. He did, however, possess a magic hammer. Using that, he conjured up veil after diaphanous veil, in which he swathed himself from head to foot and masked his face as well. The woman, creeping back again, failed to recognize him as the person who had previously chased her from the stage. She was polite to this new and rather cloudlike performer, and willingly acceded to his suggestion that they party together. The devil then used his hammer to conjure up plenty of rice wine and a wide red drinking bowl. He drank, and drank again, and yet again. But the woman, alerted by his greedy behaviour, only pretended to drink along with him. The lights seemed to go out, one by one, inside the devil's veil-swathed head. Beneath his huge limbs, as it were, a mudbox gaped open. He soon lapsed into deep stupor. The woman thereupon, with extreme caution, filched the magic hammer from his belt. And slowly, slowly, after that, she stooped to strip veil after veil from the supernatural and yet insensate lout. Then, with a peremptory handclap, she dared to awaken him. The devil rose up to find himself exposed. He rushed in rage upon the woman, for he meant to rend her limb from limb. She, however, tremblingly avoided him.

Three times he attacked her; three times she was not there.

He made a fourth and final lunge, but now the woman was ready for him. She had a few beans, sacred ones, which she had been saving to sow in spring, and some of these she now flung straight into the devil's face. He somersaulted backwards, in astonishment and pain, then drooped like a doused match and left the stage. At which point, the woman whirled and showered the audience, too, with beans. Laughing, I managed to catch a few, which I ate on the spot . . .

Ten years ago, or thereabouts, a fisherman of Mount Athos in Greece told me about Karoulia. It lies beneath a tiny anchorage in a curtain of cliffs, near the Holy Mountain's southernmost tip. Monks who have grown extremely old and sanctified retire to Karoulia, the fisherman said. Their average age, if he could be believed, is over one hundred. They live like birds, on ledges along the cliff.

'Is anyone there now?' I asked.

'Of course. I'll run you down in my boat if you like. You may even see him.'

'Who?'

'Him. Simon. A very holy person.'

The next morning was calm, serene. The fisherman and I dropped down the coast in his squat little boat, past Dionysiou. We anchored without difficulty, in under the cliff. Footholds had been cut in the rock. Chains hung from spikes driven in beside the steps. The chains and steps together made a zigzag pattern overhead. One wire cut straight down across them to the anchorage, like a sword stroke. I asked the fisherman what that was for. 'The holy Simon', he said, 'sends his basket down on that wire. When we come by this way we put something into the basket for him to eat. It's not here today, though. That means he's fasting.'

'Would it be all right for me to disturb him at such a time?'

The fisherman shrugged. 'If those chains will hold you, it is as God wills.'

So I started climbing up alone, hanging on to the chains. It was hard going. After a while I thought fatigue and vertigo would do me in. Then I reached the point of no return. I knew I lacked the strength to about-face and climb all the way down again; so I pressed on. I reached a broad ledge, finally, and pulled myself up onto it. There I lay gasping like a landed fish, prone, profoundly incurious, staining the rock with sweat. Then I sensed that someone stood over me; his shadow felt cool across my shoulders. I turned onto my back. Sparkling-eyed, erect, nearly toothless, and like a skeleton, Simon spread his arms wide.

'Oristé!' he said, meaning 'Welcome! What can I do for you?' The Greek word also connotes the horizon, appropriately.

Simon welcomed me to a fresh-made world. The sea, the sun, the rock, the man himself, seemed to have stepped through to existence a moment before. They were new-born; I was the old one. Dumbly I rose. The hermit took my hand and led me

71

along the ledge to a little garden of earth which he had inserted in a lip of the rock. He showed his few rows of struggling, growing greenery. I made no comment. They were tomato plants, I imagine, as I look back. Simon drew me on into a tiny rock chapel which he had built. Above the altar stood a framed cheap lithograph of the Virgin and Child. The hermit invited me to pray, and afterwards he brought me into his cave cell. It was a clean, dim, tidy room. He made me sit just like an honoured guest, in the one chair. I was still tongue-tied, completely. I felt like some clumsy grown-up at a child's make-believe tea. This would be my only chance, I guessed, to speak with someone so human, so advanced as Simon. I longed to question him, yet not one question came to mind. I simply could not speak to such a one. I was afraid that if I said a word some subtle vermin visible to him would pop out of my mouth. Yet even that, I think, would not have surprised or upset Simon. He took my silence with attentive calm. 'Please consider', he seemed to say, 'that you and I are here at a love feast, a real party.' Somewhere he found a caramel candy. This he put by itself on a saucer, and ceremoniously offered to me.

I hesitated, I suppose, before accepting the candy. Then as I raised it to my lips a dreary sense of the practical world returned to me. I had not thought to bring a gift for the hermit. His bones showed; they seemed ready to break through the parchment skin. He needed nourishment, as I myself did not. Thinking these things, I palmed the caramel. Surreptitiously, I slipped it underneath the saucer for him to find later. Then I got up, bowed as low as I could, and hurried out, away, over the ledge. I swung down the long chains towards the anchorage.

The sun was just setting when I arrived. The fisherman sprawled on his boatdeck, asleep. I stripped off my clothes and stepped into the pink and crystal water. I floated out around the boat, turned on my back and gazed up at the sky. A distant hum came down to me. It grew into a kind of shriek, descending swiftly, as if to attack! But I could see nothing coming. Numb with terror, I let myself sink. I swam underwater into the shadow of the boat. There I surfaced, and looked up warily. The wire which cut diagonally down across the cliff was vibrating. A string hung loosely curled along the wire. That, I felt sure, had not been there before. And then I realized what must have occurred. Simon had let his basket slide noisily down the wire, on purpose. Yes, there lay the basket. It was a high-sided pannier of straw, leaning against the iron spike to which the wire was anchored. Splashing ashore, I peered inside. My candy had come back! I put the caramel straight into my mouth. And like a child once more I tasted its burnt sugar elixir right down to my toes.

Never before in this life, possibly, had my poor spirit taken nourishment. I stood dripping upon the shore of time, and Simon waved to me from eternity.

Mercy

Closing my eyes, I cut across the years through cactus fields, to an adobe hut. I lay inside there, stretched out on a bed, watching a Mexican girl put down the tattered green window-shade. She was perhaps twenty years old, yet already heavy in the breasts and hips. Needles of sunlight pierced the well-worn shade. The girl removed her slip. In this light she was tallow-coloured, with flowing scratches from the needles of sun. She squatted down to yank open a dresser drawer. Her heavy black braids brushed the mud floor as she stooped low with her back to me, earnestly fumbling for something in the drawer.

My eyes wandered to the art reproduction in a tin frame of a flowery kind which stood on her bedside table. It represented the Virgin of Guadalupe, haloed with light upon a mountain, red rosebuds snowing down. Just a few hundred miles up the road at that moment, in the Archbishop's garden at Santa Fe, my mother was writing the legend of Guadalupe. It told how the Virgin showed herself to a peasant named Juan, as he was on his way to fetch a doctor for a dying man. The vision did not keep him long, but ordered him to build a church – impossible command! That miraculous fall of roses, however, made it possible for Juan. They fell by the armful, it seemed. At the same time, their images were steeping the Virgin's garment. Juan got the church built to house it. Relic and church remain, Mother wrote, as outward signs of the Virgin's continuing mercy . . .

The girl drew something from the drawer, stood up, and faced me once again. Her lips were twitching uncertainly. A nickle-plated revolver gleamed in her warm brown hand. 'My husband,' she explained in a small voice, 'he may come home!' She aimed straight at my heart. I lay rigid, speechless with fright. The girl herself shuddered, and then like some reluctant false-penis her weapon drooped. My hand reached down and closed around a coca-cola bottle underneath the bed. Leaping erect, I waved the bottle in her face.

'Point that pistol again', I hissed at her, being insane with rage, relief, and lust also, 'and I will break your wrist!'

Incredibly enough, we made armed truce, belly to belly, furious, with our weapons not relinquished but still gripped in our fists throughout the performance. The so-called husband, real or not, never turned up. The end of the day proved peaceful, after all; we parted friends. But I was uneasy; she frightened me still, and no doubt the reverse was true as well. That night I moved on to another town.

A month or so later, north of Mexico, I fell for a Ute Indian girl. She was spontaneous and supple as a swimming eel, but bound in marriage to a jealous gambler. One evening I spirited her away in my car, deep into the holy silence of the desert. There was a flat-topped outcropping of sandstone she knew about, some forty feet in height, with a crevice in it which formed a natural staircase. Together, we scrambled up. Feeling safe at the top, we spread our clothes for cushioning and then proceeded to fulfil every desire we shared as darkness fell.

Along about midnight, another car came roaring in our direction along the bumpy track. We both sat up to look, and instantly ducked down again. The car's headlights seemed intent on seeking us out. We heard the car brake to a stop not far from the place where we ourselves had parked. Very cautiously, I raised myself to peer once more over the edge. Like dragon wings, the car doors creaked open. Three men emerged, muttering amongst themselves. They slouched across to the base of the rock. That was when I remembered the round boulder resting near the top of the crevice which served as a staircase up. I crawled across to it. The boulder was heavy but nicely balanced, it moved beneath my hand. I thought I ought to wait until my enemies had climbed about halfway. Cramped in the crevice they would then be unable to dodge my heaven-sent missile. I felt no qualms. They say that certain beasts of prey regard themselves as being like men. I was a mountain lion then. The girl had crawled across to clamp her arms about my knees. What was she whispering?

'Please don't kill anyone!'

I pushed her off. The men should have begun climbing by now. Instead, they stood and talked. Fiercely, quietly, I leaned out over the rock face to listen. At the same moment, they fell silent. Then came a sound, soft, unexpected. The men were pissing against the cliff. Oblivious, they finished, zipped up once more and went back to their car. The machine growled into gear. It lurched on down the track towards Medicine Hat.

I cried like a baby. So did the girl, cringing away from me. The night was billion-eyed with stars, each one of which had witnessed the full murder in my coward heart . . .

Stone lanterns, glimmering between the trees, illuminated each path leading up the hill. At every turning or crossing of the paths, bonfires tossed their sparkling arms towards the stars. At the top of the hill was a temple pavilion in the shelter of an immense and very ancient pine. The thick trunk and contorted limbs of the pine twisted like flames. Its dark masses of needles appeared magnetized, they were so motionless. The pavilion was illuminated by iron braziers fed with crackling pine-knots. Yellow ripples of light swirled over the plank floor.

A kneeling man put a drum to his shoulder. A second musician set a drum in the crook of his arm. The men yowled softly. They struck the drums now and again. A small flute shrilled. Robed in blood and brilliancy, and masked in gold, and lightly, with a gliding motion of infinite slowness, spirits of the dead appeared. They spread their fans . . .

It seemed that a monkey was circling the earth in a space satellite. The animal had been trained to perform certain chores in orbit. These automatically triggered rewards: its nourishment. But now for some reason the creature out there had ceased to care. It was 'falling down on the job', the television newscaster explained. The scientists back at the space station had been reduced to triggering the monkey's food and drink by radio. 'My own idea', the newscaster concluded, 'is that the animal has figured out how to get fed without working. So it takes advantage, just like human beings!'

The next morning, buttons were pressed. The space monkey hurtled home. Somewhere in Texas, they opened its capsule. The animal hopped out and made a reverent little monkey bow, as if to announce itself. Announce itself to whom? Was it to the scientists, or was it to our common mother? The monkey straightened up again, scratched, blinked uncertainly, and toppled over on the grass. Stone cold dead it was. The creature's heart had stopped. 'Unaccountably', as the saying goes.

Who am I? What am I? And for what purpose? Perhaps questions like these occurred to the monkey out in black space. And possibly they put him in such mental pain as to cause death; who knows? In any case, the news died with the animal.

A day or two afterwards, 'Apollo Eleven' lifted off. Henry Grunwald, my editor of the moment, flew down to Cape Canaveral to witness that historic moon-shot. By cocktail time, he was back in his office overlooking the Avenue of the Americas. Manhattan's skyscrapers had been sizzling like curling irons in the heat of the afternoon. Now a violent thunderstorm hosed them down. Henry and I stood with our foreheads pressed to his plate glass, gazing down into the suddenly darkened avenue. Stalled traffic gleamed like tulip beds set in soaking black tar far below. I was talking about the death of the monkey. 'It sounds like a coincidence,' Henry remarked.

Just then, although we did not know it at the time, Manhattan seized up. In the subway tunnels below Lexington Avenue, the lights went out. Screeching, the trains swam to a halt. They had been swamped by the downpour above. The train doors automatically jammed. A hundred thousand creatures of the crush hour sweated and screamed, in pitch darkness. Breaking windows, they began a mass struggle to reach the street. Some never made it. They died in the steaming rock bowels of the island. Meanwhile priests, kneeling on the pavement, shouted *Extreme Unction* down through the iron grates . . .

It helps to listen to the dead, especially in the morning when you first wake up. They are going to sleep then, as it were, leaving their thoughts with you.

Let them come through.

Intelligence

'Thou shalt not kill.' The commandment is as explicit in Buddhism as it is in Christianity, and has been ignored in the same way. Here in Japan, for example, from the very beginning, Zen-Buddhism has been linked to *bushido* – the Way of the Warrior. The martial arts, so-called, of sword and bow, were and are imparted by Zen masters and dead-seriously pursued. It is true that we now possess far 'better' weapons with which to wound and destroy one another – meaning ourselves, of course. We make, and we trade back and forth, swords which can slash humanity in half, and poisoned arrows capable of collapsing this planet's atmosphere like a pricked balloon. Our fantasy life, meanwhile, revolves very largely upon the shark-toothed fascination of the vortex. As a race, in short, we seem suicide-bent. This everybody knows, and no one can prevent.

I once described the writer Norman Mailer as a poetical – and not political – animal. He wanted to know what I meant by that. 'It's no crack,' I told him. 'For such as you to seek political power is like some benighted swan trying to put on weight and roar like the lion.'

'Clout is what I want,' Mailer rejoined. 'You've had your

beak in there; you know what I mean, don't you?' With that, he got up on his toes and glared into my eyes. Nonplussed for a moment, I glared back down at him. We seemed frozen into a stock tableau – 'eyeball to eyeball', as the saying is.

'It's all power,' Mailer muttered to me under his breath. 'There's nothing else but power.'

I laughed. Yet then I thought: Look at him strut! He's so rich, so successful after all. Perhaps Mailer has a point, at that. He, with his mailed foot in his velvet mouth.

Soon afterwards I visited Geoffrey Blunden in Paris. We stepped out onto Blunden's balcony, overlooking the Rue Saint-Jacques. During the Sorbonne student riots there had been a struggle for a barricade in the street below our feet. His own teen-age children were involved, he told me, pointing down. The police had used tear-gas on them.

'What was it all about?' I asked.

'Power.'

'That's something everybody seems to be after,' I said. 'Should writers also seek power?'

Geoff drily laughed. I waited. Unbelievingly, he turned to look at me. His eyes were round, surprised-looking. His lips, as often seems to be the case with eloquent men, were tense and thin. It struck me that his face, with its curtain of rumpled hair, resembled a sad and stubborn old ram's.

'All right,' I said after a minute. 'I withdraw the question.'

Geoff shrugged: 'Power is no joking matter. It belongs to the beasts of prey. They won't give it away.'

'*D'accord*,' I said.

'Oh Lord, release me from this floating prison,' Father Noah cried out of the Ark, 'for I am sick because of the stench of lions!' That is our position too, wherever we may happen to reside. 'The state is an evil monster,' Friedrich Nietzsche warned, meaning governments in general. The German philosopher revealed a great and terrible secret there. Not long since, feeling in a careless mood, I communicated Nietzsche's remark to an American observer in Kyoto, a putative 'student of political science' whom I had reason to believe was a secret agent. I sought to annoy him, a little, and possibly to draw him out a bit, but no such luck. He agreed readily with what I said. Great institutions will do anything, however evil, he explained, in order to maintain their own existences. Such is the nature of the beast. And then, for whatever reason it may have been, he handed me a drink which made me ill indeed . . .

Best not mess with the ignorant armies of 'intelligence'! The trouble is, they mess, unasked, with practically everyone. This has become common knowledge of late, and yet the chances are that nothing can change it. There are too many jobs at stake, around the world; too many have been recruited already. Those who refused to be recruited, moreover, or who presumed to criticize C.I.A. methods in particular, have all been laid under suspicion and thought to bear watching at one time or another. No matter that their own interests might be light-years removed from the blood-red-carpeted corridors of power! So it was in my own case, I suppose. When I stayed at the Shelton Hotel in New York my phone was bugged. My home phone in Rome was tapped when I was filming at the Vatican. I have been followed and photographed in various world capitals – instances of unnecessary surveillance which make me itch to think about. Once in Prague, at the National Museum, a muscle-bound operative devoted a whole day to watching me study a painting by Pieter Bruegel. At closing-time he ventured a question: 'You like?' I nodded unhappily. Bruegel himself, I was tempted to tell the man, had often been under scrutiny by the secret police of his own distant day. What did they see?

A dark spring morning in the small hill town of Vézelay, in France, comes back to me. In the ancient basilica, ladders were leaning everywhere, and stone dust whitely drifting on the gelid air. Masons in paper caps and coarse wool sweaters laboured with trowels to shore up the crumbling columns. The basilica was closed for repairs, but even so they let me wander about at will. I had come a long way to see the capitals of the columns in particular: those fabulous relics of the romanesque, rich in bas-relief lions. Samson was wrestling with one lion. Another gave a ride to David the shepherd boy. The prophet Daniel, sitting serenely enthroned in stone petals of light, made me think of Sakyamuni. Demons had gathered round to share in the Buddha's enlightenment; a pride of lions prowled the periphery of Daniel's bliss. The poet William Blake said that the wrath of the lion is the wisdom of God, or words to that effect.

Right here at Vézelay, I remembered, Richard Coeur-de-lion marshalled his crusaders for the Holy Land. The masons now knocked off for lunch: bread, garlic, cheese and wine. One man had a transistor radio; he turned it on. A rattle of news and static swept like fine hail through the basilica. After a while, one of the listeners got up and walked over to where I stood. He shook my hand. There was commiseration in his voice as he announced:

'*Votre King est mort!*'

Uncomprehendingly, I gaped.

'*Oui, oui, c'est vrai,*' the man explained. '*Votre Martin Luther King, assassiné.*'

Yet another crusader crucified . . .

The first time I visited Jerusalem, the Holy Rock stood within Jordan. An Arab policeman was assigned to keep an eye on me. We climbed the cobbled alleys past the Wailing Wall to the sacred enclosure on the crest of the Rock. Removing our shoes, the policeman and I first entered the mosque which is called Al Aqsa.

'The name means "Far Away",' the policeman explained. 'One night Mohammed the Prophet came to this place, in a flash, from a great distance. The angel Gabriel stood guard over his horse, which was made out of lightning. The Rock itself, this holy Mount Moriah, lifted up to help Mohammed enter heaven at that moment. But the Prophet gently put the mountain back down beneath his hand.'

Stepping outside again, we went and sat on a wall with some blind men. The cypresses stood before us like black exhalations of the parchment-coloured earth. 'Do you mean to say,' I asked the policeman, 'that Mount Moriah was alive in Mohammed's time?'

'Oh, yes. It used to rear twelve miles into the air. By day, its shadow fell on Jericho. By night, a ruby the size of a lion used to shine from here. The four Rivers of Paradise – Sihon, Bihon, Nile and Euphrates – flowed from this terrace. Not only that, but the Dome of the Rock which you see over there was plated with pure gold. A sheath of skins, like a huge foreskin, used to be pulled up over it in rough weather. We had a hundred and fifty Jews washing and sweeping the entire shrine down every day. The carpetbeaters for it were Christian, you know, in better times. But the future will witness still more wonderful things. Mount Moriah will be transformed into white coral when the Day of Judgment comes. It is to be God's throne.'

'Will Jesus attend the Last Judgment?'

'No doubt of it. He was a great prophet. Look over there. Do you see that stone cradle? Jesus used to lie in it and prophesy when he was a little baby.'

'It looks to me like a stone mortar', I said, 'for grinding wheat. Maybe you've got Jesus mixed up with Adonis, a god of vegetation.'

The policeman looked shocked. To change the subject, I pointed to an exquisite small shrine nearby: 'And what does that commemorate?'

'The Chain of Truth,' he said. 'In King Solomon's time, a blue steel chain hung straight down out of heaven to that spot. Whoever told the truth, could hold onto the chain. Whoever lied, would see it fly up out of reach. Solomon seemed wise because he tested each case by the Chain of Truth. So things went on, until one day an Arab moneylender came to sue a Jew for nonpayment of debt. The Jew swore up and down that he had already returned the Arab's money. This was true in a sense. What he had done was to hide the money, for a trick, inside the Arab's bamboo walking stick. So the Arab, innocently waving his cane, swore that he had received nothing.'

'What happened?' I asked.

'What do you think? The chain got disgusted with them both, and flew away.'

'Well,' I said, 'times change.'

'They do, and then again they do not. Right underneath us, inside the Rock, is a huge reservoir which we call the Cistern of the Leaf. Solomon quarried it out. A man named Shuraik ibn-Habashah went down there once on a routine inspection tour, by boat of course. He got lost in the cavern, turned a corner unexpectedly, and entered the Garden of Paradise. There he stayed, for an eternity of bliss. But in the end he wanted to revisit Jerusalem. He plucked a leaf from the Garden, and returned as he had come. Only a moment of Jerusalem time had passed. He never found the door to Paradise again, but the leaf of the Garden which he brought back never, never withered.'

'What colour was it?'

'The colour of dried blood with golden veins, on the top of the leaf, and black with veins of silver underneath. It used to be kept in the Caliph's treasury, but now it's disappeared . . . Sir, what religion did you say you were?'

'I belong to no church.'

'Poor fish!'

'Yes,' I said. 'I'm a fish that neither drinks nor drowns.'

For a minute or two the policeman wrestled with his own thoughts. He sat hunched over, clutching the bulge of his muscular stomach. His eyes, half shut against the sunlight, avoided mine.

'Are you ill?' I asked.

'Yes, no . . . a little nervous indigestion.' He rose resignedly: 'I can't keep you from looking at the Wailing Wall, unless you're Jewish. So, let's go. It is right below.'

We went down by a cobbled alleyway strewn with garbage. The stones of the Wall are huge, irregular in shape, and so joined as to interlock. They are not mortared together. I noticed grass and a few wild flowers growing between the stones. A handful of Arab children were playing ball, bouncing their ball off the Wall. As the policeman and I approached, the eldest child slapped the littlest one hard across the face. Then they all ran away screaming. The policeman stood back and scratched himself.

I stepped close to the Wall, touched it, looked up, touched it again, feeling a momentary vertigo. Moriah seemed to slide beneath my fingertips. I was remembering Crusader days. In 1099, I think it was, Tancred and his friends butchered every man, woman and child in Jerusalem. After the massacre, Raymond of Anguillers went to inspect the noble sanctuary on the crest of the Rock. He reported having to wade between islands of corpses in a lake of blood. For some days after that the Crusaders worked full time to cart away flyblown flesh and scrub up drying gore. Then, says a contemporary account, 'they donned fresh clothes and walked barefooted, sighing and weeping, through the Holy Places of the city where Jesus Christ the Saviour of the world trod in the flesh. And they gently kissed the flagstones where His feet had pressed.'

No, the Holy Rock is no hiding place.

Yume

Daitokuji temple has suffered a stormy history. A man named Takuan, who lived in the seventeenth century, was the 153rd Chief Abbot to take it in hand. Takuan freely gave advice to swordsmen, calligraphers, ink-painters, potters, tea-masters and Noh-dramatists. He was chary, however, of teaching religion, and never pretended that anyone had gained Zen-mastery from him. When the time came for Takuan to die, his monks gathered round the sickbed and begged him to compose a final farewell poem. Tradition called for him to do it, but Takuan would not consent. Instead, with one finger, he reluctantly traced a single Chinese character on the bedclothes. Through tear-dimmed eyes, his monks peered at the sign which he made.

Of all his generation, Takuan had seemed to be the person most prodigiously energetic, alert, and wide-awake. Yet now his slowly moving finger traced nothing but *Yume*, which means 'dream'. Did that refer to what was past, or passing, or to come for Takuan? The past, doubtless, because, brief and lonely though it may seem, life does pass like a thronged interminable dream.

The present, however, must have been in it too, for Takuan in his death-struggle resembled a fish in a landing-net: the sleep-heavy mesh of mind with body. As for the future, who could say? *Yume* once more, perhaps. Yet Takuan's religion taught and still teaches today that one can awaken from the dream that was, the dream that is, and even from the dream that will be in time. Life itself is a dream, according to Zen-Buddhism, not because it is hopeless but just the reverse. Life is essentially a transition process from heavy sleep to full awakening and hence dream-like . . .

Turn a street-corner in New York, upon a time, and I was on my own. I had freedom from observation, a luxury now. Okay, when no one seemed to be looking, what would I do? Pop into a White Rose Bar, possibly, to purchase the 25-cent *Large Vodka* which could make everything magic for a while. Then, I might just watch the pigeons in Central Park. The sooty plumes of their erratically bobbing necks flashed royal purple and spring green. Beautiful city birds, they barely noticed me. To them I must have seemed either a dim heavy divinity or a torpid and inscrutable animal – I'll never know. But now they say that pigeons too are being trained to spy, made part of mankind's worldwide war-upon-ourselves-kit.

Leaving the park again, I might buy a pack of Pall Malls from one of those vending machines with mirrors on the front. My upper lip on the left, and the first two fingers of my right hand, were nicotine-stained. What else would the mirror have shown? A happy, glassy-eyed stranger on the loose, halfway anaesthetized with booze, but really high on his own sex-drive.

At first, New York spelled freedom. Year by year, however, it seemed to close in. When my employer put up a new sky-scraper with every window sealed, the end approached. A tiny accident tipped the balance. Pacing my air-conditioned cell one day, in socks as usual, I happened to tread upon a tack. It hurt a bit. More to the point was that it worried me, for I was some-thing of a hypochondriac. After an hour or so of fretting off and on, I took the elevator down to the twentieth-floor infirmary. I expected to get a soothing smile from the nurse in charge, together with a dab of iodine. But everything had changed, I found; there were three nurses now, all ugly, and a couple of severe young doctors prowling the background. No one there had anything to do, and so it was not long before the entire staff stood zeroed in on my little problem. The question, as they all saw it, was: what had I been doing with my shoes off? 'Custom,' I explained, lamely enough.

'Don't joke with us, mister. This won't look very nice on your record, you know.'

Speechless, it came to me that I had been brought to birth in a thicket of ultramarine, washed in springwater from a silver pitcher, and dried with a crimson cloth. The four corners of my cradle were night and day, sunrise and sunset, surely. But in the darkness of the womb I had seen more. Yes, in the womb I looked on gleefully while sun-yellow and shadow-blue wrestled together for my sake alone. Like *sumo* champions, or the gables of a well-built house which the hurricane rocks, they leaned shoulder to shoulder with their arms tight-locked, straining until sweat streaked their sides like chains of eyes. Beneath their feet, green sprang like grass, while overhead their violet and orange pinions crossed to create vermilion, the blood-red poppy of the rock.

Was that all fantasy, or what? The ugly old nurses and the severe young doctors looked reproving still, or shocked, like death in white, I thought. I laughed, rudely enough, and they took me to task for that as well. But I had made up my mind, meanwhile, to leave the company. Next stop: Europe. Greener pastures, I guessed, and rightly so.

But now, wherever we may travel, the hydrogen sulphide fumes from the jaws of nations are stifling us. The monsters which humanity has made and loosely chained up in the bunks of this planetary Ark are slavering and snarling and spewing and praying for peace and performing weapons-tests in their bedpans and biting when and where they can, while earth sours, the sea bleeds, and the air itself winces with sharp disgust.

Buried within humanity, as in a living grave, God appears powerless to reverse the evil that we do.

Originally I accepted what was taught in school; my brain believed in escape through progress, call it evolution. As to the source of the whole continuing story, my teachers said that was found in the sun – a thing not to be looked at, for it blinds. Still, my heart questioned this, beating with doubt. What is the food of the sun? And has that anything to do with us, after all? We burn in heaven, I think now. We seize, we bind; we are captured at the same time and inextricably entwined. We ourselves partake less of the light than of the darkness which knows it not.

A pebble in a stream reflects light, but light is internal too. A diamond seems to demonstrate this paradox; so does a burning coal. Everything we experience, in fact, keeps on giving away its light and heat. In physical theory there may exist 'black holes' which do just the reverse, but that is a matter for speculation alone.

'People look at flowers', a Chinese sage of the Taoist persuasion was once heard to complain, 'as if they were in a dream.' True, but flowers are not dreaming; each bespeaks its inner light. With animals, however, evolution takes a new and astonishing turn. The light that is in them wavers, half-drowned in the tidal surging of attraction-repulsion, hunger and satiety. And finally in human beings the same emotional breakers burst in the form of seething mist; they become consciousness, which obscures almost everything.

Minerals/plants/animals/people. Is this really an evolutionary process, or is it the reverse? Involution, involution of light, perhaps. Not God (as our ancestors thought) but Man, has hidden himself, as in a dream, or cloud: *Yume.*

I myself keep on trying to awaken through *zazen*, or, failing that, to build a little will-power, like heat in the belly, remembering the Zen-Buddhist vow which we novices regularly intone in Japanese. It is a fourfold promise to achieve what we cannot, a mindless challenge which we children chirp to the moveless rock face of the unfathomable. In English translation, it might run:

'However innumerable are the creatures and things peculiar to this world, I vow to save one and all. However inexhaustible the passions I have undergone and will and do undergo, I vow to overcome them one and all. However immeasurable the guiding Dharma-laws which steer the entire universe from within, I vow to comprehend each and all in myself. However incomparable, unique and hence forever solitary be the true Buddha-nature, I vow to embrace it with all my heart and thereby to become Buddha in turn.'

The actual Japanese is sonorous, but less replete with verbal flourishes. 'I do whole-heartedly bend my will to the impossible, to over-coming, embracing and incorporating four-fold infinity!' That is what it comes down to. One begins each sitting thus. In the *zendo*, the *zazen* practice hall, one is expected to be explicitly absurd . . .

Long ago, according to legend, a sage named Hermes Trismegistus stood with his son Tat on a mountain-top over-looking the Sinai desert, and suggested that they search out something together without stirring from the rock which supported their feet at that moment. 'What are we supposed to find, Father?' Tat inquired.

'That which is undefiled, unlimited, without form, without colour, nude, gleaming, and for you alone to discover.'

'Father, this is not like any teaching I have heard from you before. I feel quite incapable, and worse. Am I still sane?'

'Until this moment, my son, I could not expect you to perceive a thing which is neither dry nor wet, neither hard nor soft, neither cuttable nor uncuttable, and neither bound nor free. But now if you will draw this nothing and this everything to yourself, keeping holy silence, filled with desire, it will become you.'

They stood silent then, from sunrise until noon, when suddenly Tat cried out: 'My Father, I am in heaven, in the earth, in air, in water, everywhere. I am in plants and animals as well, hearing what they grow, feeling what they say. Tell me, Father, about this new body which with your help I have put on. It seems to be composed of energies alone. Will this ever perish?'

'Never, for this lives by dying. Do you not know that you were born a god, and a son of One, just as I have been?'

Every image of Buddha in meditation silently speaks to the pilgrim who has ears to hear the unspoken. And this is true even of the most vast, impressive images which have been created in Buddha's name. The one at Todaiji, for instance, some fifty feet high. No bo tree casts its shade upon that upright rounded mountain of bronze, but a thousand-petalled lotus supports the Buddha's giant thighs. The petals appear to blossom and fall like small waves all around him, each one engraved with images of other Buddhas, other worlds, through which the timeless One radiates endlessly.

The Cloistered Emperor Shomu dedicated that statue back in the eighth century, whereupon the native gods and goddesses of Japan were seen to rally round. The ancient female deity of the sun, for one, declared through oracles and dreams that *she* was the Buddha. Then ten thousand fierce monks escorted Hachiman, the Shinto god of war, from his ancestral home at Usa all the way to Todaiji. His eight-bannered carriage drew up at the temple. The war god's image precariously swayed forth to bow before Sakyamuni in Meditation. What did who see? If Buddha had stood up to greet his guest, the temple roof would have been destroyed, and possibly the morning star revealed once more.

At Todaiji, the other day, I tossed ten yen into the offering-box, and banged the gong below the precipice of Buddha's knee. This was in deference to custom, for good luck; yet Buddha frowned, I thought. Huge, menacing now, he squeezed his third eye shut. I lit a candle in his honour, but the wind whipping in through the wide open doorway blew it out again. And at that moment something came drifting down to me like a spark from the couch-size curve of Sakyamuni's cast-bronze lips:

'Freedom,' I thought he said. 'Images have it not, but you are free.'

Am I, though? This question, along with the premature summer heat tonight, makes me sweat. All right; my body sweats and my lower ego, if I may call it so, appears abashed. My Western education however, especially in Rudolph Steiner's Anthroposophy, leads me to accept after all the whispered word of the image at Todaiji. There is in me a 'higher ego' which can *kushu*, for example, some koans set by tradition and by life itself. Indeed I have a partner who translates the essentially untranslatable word *kushu* by means of 'ego' used as a verb. One cannot solve the riddles of the universe; true enough. Yet it is not impossible 'to ego' some of them in the freedom of inmost within-ness.

East, West, North, South, wherever one may look today, one sees new beginnings of such joyous work and infinitely difficult play. We can witness the budding of planetary consciousness. Not only that, but partake in it.

PART THREE *Summer*

Which way?
The radish-picker points
with his radish.

KOBAYASHI ISSA

Sand-Castles

INDIA provided the initial body of Buddhist literature, but Chinese artists, poets and hermits added an element of freedom. An independent daily life, the ancient Chinese fathers of Zen-Buddhism believed, is the main thing to cultivate. That, plus 'looking into one's ordinary mind'. Subsequently, the Japanese capped Chinese sense with spirit of an arduously dedicated kind. Being organization-prone, like coiled springs often enough, they brought new control to the Zen impulse. Now, what will America and Europe in turn contribute? This religious movement keeps on growing, flowing eastward across the centuries, and so the question is not altogether an idle one. Besides, there is a negative case to make against certain specifically Japanese aspects of Zen-Buddhism. Here monastery training is quasi-military, with motionless drill in place of the close-order variety, and plenty of brutally hard beatings administered, but it does come to an end. Most monks stay a few years at most, before scattering to work in the world or returning to temples which they are due to inherit. Sad to say, very few of them gain *satori*.

'East is East and West is West, and never the twain shall meet! In other words your poet Rudyard Kipling had it right!' The Japanese official who told me that had taken a postgraduate degree at Columbia University in New York, and spent some years stationed in Paris. We were sitting together in one of Kyoto's hundreds of Italian-style coffee-shops, listening to tape-recorded Kentucky Blue Grass music. So he just had to be joking, I thought. Unfortunately, I laughed out loud. His eyes glanced sharply up from his coffee, and then skidded away again. He should have known, that look said plainly, that I could not be trusted with the truth of his discouragement.

The strange thing is that most Westerners in Kyoto take the same position. Japanese acquaintances, they often complain, regard them as guests rather than brothers under the skin. Kyoto's conformist and nostalgic atmosphere depresses them. A former automobile salesman from the Detroit area told me that he could hardly wait to get home to the 'fee world', as he called it, where things have their price in paper money rather than formalities and restrictions. But how about my own view? Would I care to fly home to a high nest of dollar bills, or would I rather retain this present precarious perch upon a folded paper fan? On balance, I shall stay for a while longer, despite the fact that from the Zen-Buddhist point of view sticking to anything at all – even to clinglessness – is heresy of a kind. 'Break your habits!' the Zen masters insist. 'Blast your own beliefs! Kill Buddha!'

But is such a thing possible? What if there actually exists, as Aristotle for one assumed, an 'Unmoved Mover' behind everything that moves? Logic so demands, and heavenly phenomena such as the Pole Star seem to body forth human ideas of that which is pure and forever still. Few Christians have felt inclined to quarrel with Aristotle. His 'Unmoved Mover' is God, they suppose. Yet there have been heretics, the Manicheans in particular, who taught that what turns everything around is not God but a devilish 'Archon' – a perverted child of Desire, who only thinks he created the world which he so cruelly stirs. The so-called Secret Book of John, for example, maintains that the First Archon chained up the stars of heaven, the daemons, and mankind alike, through measure and motion, so that one and all fell into Fate's fetters – 'an evil and tortuous plan'. Such language reflects an age that is gone, but not the thought behind it. Modern cosmologists in the ranks of science can do without the notion of an Archon to screw things up tight, or so they may suppose, but none the less their orthodoxy merely presents the old grey nightmare in a new form. Namely, determinism. And this, in my opinion, is what we must slay if we can.

Determinism is making sand-castles of modern philosophy – and of religions, too. All religions, Zen-Buddhism among the rest, are subject to what once was called religious heresy. All are crumbling in determinism's undertow. That being true, why fool with religion? Is it because I sense myself to be a free radical particle of human consciousness in general? I dare to presume that a microsecond's spirit-dash, off-course and in part painful yes, might contribute in ways *not* yet determined to the whole incalculable evolution of God from Man. If that is so, then I must not indulge in self-pity. Human consciousness *is* suffering; so much for its shadow-side. Positively, it is playful, and creative as well as ruinous. Play, not Fate, steers the universe from within . . .

To create, or to destroy, means beginning over again at the start; and there is no other way but this, in religion or out of it. Determinism, however, is based on the belief that no beginning is possible; everything must follow from causes already set. The causal links in the reasoning process itself, as well as in nature, prove as much from the determinist viewpoint. However, one need not see things that way. A log of wood does not burn to ashes in the fireplace, except theoretically. Seen with an artist's eye – which is to say with normal human vision – it is first a log of wood, then fire, and finally ashes. Which is the right view? To use your head is bad and good; to use your eyes is good and bad. Lao Tsu taught that one ought not to think about such things but let them play along in the silence which the mind overlooks. The mind is like a house with a beautiful view, he once remarked. Forget housework, sit on the porch, and rock.

Lao Tsu's gentle injunctions played, through Taoism, into Zen. The thirteenth-century Zen missionary named Dogen, whose thought Masao Abe helps to preserve and propagate, preached the necessity of 'dropping both body and mind'. But all too often this is treated as a task – a practically impossible task, at that – rather than getting out of work and into play.

The Zen establishment naturally has tried to keep up with the changing times. Both before and during the Second World War, for instance, it diligently trained officer cadres. Japan's defeat plunged Zen into local eclipse for a brief spell, but soon the new big corporation bosses found how useful it could be for conditioning recruits to their management ranks. At present, one in three Japanese firms inculcate their own brands of business *bushido* by means of deliberate brainwashing. Fuji Bank, for instance, puts three thousand new employees annually through a one-year course in sacrificing self and family for the corporation's sake. Rival Fukuoka Bank sends its white-collar hopefuls to an Air Self-Defence camp where they are exhorted to emulate the *kamikaze* suicide-mission pilots who fell like crazed moths upon the advancing United States Navy in the long ago. After this, Fukuoka apprentices proceed to a Zen temple where the abbot, assisted by shouting and stick-wielding attendants, shepherds them through a long spine-cracking bout of compulsory *zazen*, with the explanation that obedience, obedience and more obedience are called for at the temple and will be demanded at the bank as well. While money calls the tune here in Japan, paralytic clackings, muffled shrieks and embarrassed hisses comprise too much of the music . . .

Long ago in China there lived a spiritual seeker named Hsiang, who had the good luck to sit at the feet of a genuine yet shamelessly loquacious Zen abbot. He took voluminous notes, naturally. When at last the abbot died, Hsiang was chosen to replace him. His first duty would be to prepare a set of lectures for the monks, so Hsiang holed up with his notes for a time. But now they all appeared rubbish to him. With a brief prayer to his old teacher for understanding and forgiveness, Hsiang burned all the sayings which he had recorded from the lips of the dead man. It was a crazy thing to do, the monks complained, and then they harried Hsiang out into the wilderness. Alone, among the mountains, Hsiang came upon an abandoned hermitage. He made it his own dwelling place, and occupied his time by sweeping up around the grave of the hermit who had lived there before himself – a man whose name he did not know. As he swept, the teachings which his former abbot had so readily lobbed into Hsiang's consciousness kept on coming back, resurfacing in his mind, much to his own annoyance and distress. So he swept harder than ever. Thus it occurred that as he flailed away at the ground his broom happened to dash a pebble against a bamboo tree. The pebble made a hollow *tch*, as it hit. That was all, yet even so the one *tch* immediately entered both of Hsiang's ears and met between his eyes like thunder, soft though the sound was, dissolving every doctrine he had ever learned, all at a single stroke. At one and the same instant of time, Hsiang gained wisdom and was struck dumb. Punishment, or reward?

The answer is silence, and a chill mist arising from the silver lake of Hsiang's latter-day transparency.

For ourselves, meanwhile, the *tch* of scientific determinism has effectively silenced most old-time religion. Our globe has shed its crowning glory; it is growing spiritually egg-bald. Yet seen through an electron microscope even an egg has hair. This newly denuded planet prickles in the solar wind.

Tree-Mother

In the shade of a maple tree in the Catskill Mountains, I lay talking with three men. The first was the fight trainer Charley Goldstein. The second was a middle-aged factory-hand who appeared prematurely exhausted. His name was Marchegiano. The centre of the group was Marchegiano's son, a heavyweight prizefighter in training. The fighter's voice was high-pitched and gentle. His handshake was as tentative as a pianist's. Yet those tanned, squarish hands of his could turn – as the whole world was soon to learn – into rib-cracking, skull-caving thunder-stones and bursting black suns. His ring name was not Marchegiano but the smoother-sounding Marciano. Everyone called him 'Rocky', or simply 'the Rock'.

'Fighting is murder,' Charley said that afternoon. 'That's why we bring the Rock on slow.'

'Why, hell,' Rocky's father put in. 'This boy is strong, but I'm stronger than him!' Kindly and boyish, bruised bronze, was the coming champion's face. He accepted his father's boast with mild good grace.

'What I like best', the Rock remarked, 'is hitting a fellow just right. I know when it happens, every time, because I feel the trill along my arm. Not only that; the guy goes down like a sack of purina. So that's the best thing can happen, of course. The next best thing, believe it or not, is when he gets to me with a hard shot. That wakes me up to fight. Besides, the other guy gets discouraged. It don't hurt me, you see.'

'The hell it don't,' Charley said. Rocky blushed red in the cool shade . . .

A dark magnificent tree lives near to me, and I walk by it almost every day. Passing beneath its branches, I acknowledge the tree's presence, of course. But that is not quite good enough. Sometimes I have the wit, or courtesy perhaps, to stop still in the shadow of this tree. I consider how earth, air, fire and water braid together here, creating and re-creating a plant-being of terrific integrity. At such times the tree seems to speak; and it helps me.

'I seem to be alone in liking to be fed by the Mother.'

The sage Lao Tsu said that. What did he mean by it? Far from being really alone, he was one among many saviours who entered the world at about the same moment in history. In China, along with Lao Tsu himself, there was Confucius. In India, Sakyamuni – or Gautama, as his countrymen knew him – the Buddha. In Greece, Socrates. These were Lao Tsu's peers. Of course all but Confucius were unknown to him. Yet no plea of ignorance need be brought to excuse Lao Tsu's complaint. It was more true than he knew. His contemporaneous peers were all pointing ahead in time, and right away from the Mother as he understood her to be.

Come down out of the Milky Way, Socrates urged, and think straight for a change. The Mother's breast is emptiness, Buddha proclaimed, and Man ought to be weaned. Confucius meanwhile preached ethics, as if morality had come before the womb. These three prophets, like Lao Tsu himself, are part of me, built into what I think and feel, yet he contradicts them.

Stone Lao Tsu; he is crazy. But the very stones turn into swallows of unreason as they are hurled, and fly away. What did he say? Probably I recall it wrong –

'The Mother is the Spirit of the Valley, the Female Principle, the Way, and she could not care less what you call her. She is infinity, inward, like white jade in a covering of rough cloth. When the Father respects and keeps watch over the Mother, he keeps relaxing back and back at the same time to become one with her and re-enter the Uncut Block.'

– something like that. His heirs naturally have been the mystics of every country, but much intervenes between them and Lao Tsu. Religion intervenes, for one thing. Philosophy, for another. And finally, profound unease about the whole female-male relationship. Lao Tsu appears to have been innocent of that unease; he was able to proclaim without embarrassment, or evidence, or proof, what seemed to him the female nature of the cosmos – all compassion – and the reconciling mission of her littlest and least offspring: tantrum-prone humanity.

Do I think Lao Tsu had it right? I don't believe he had it wrong, do I?

The nothingness coming towards me answers me. Now it stands still, in between everything. I must be careful. When I was a boy, these feelings of despair used to grow and grow until there was not even so much as vibration or mutual sympathy between the objects in my line of vision, so far as I could discern. I used to run into the woods when that occurred, and beat my head against the trees until I felt myself and my surroundings come to life again. The trees were far more comforting than wounding, I found. They never changed their minds, not drastically, nor their positions much at all, and those trees were the first Zen masters whom I knew. Pine trees, not far from the house on Paradise Road.

At Muroji the trees grow huge above the dark swift stream.

Yesterday, in gratitude to that holy place, I put my hands upon the tallest cedar there, praying without words. Not just the energy of the tree but also its steadfast quality soon played throughout my body. I felt as if I too possessed roots which descended slow and deep into the ground, while my spine seemed to be extending slowly skyward for thousands of feet. The friends who had brought me to Muroji were devotees of Noh drama, and so they understood. No explanations were required. They too touched the tree for a while, and afterwards performed a grave little dance of reverence.

Artists are not necessarily crazy to know that everything does relate after all; especially plants, animals, and mankind.

There is such a thing as subjective truth – the truth we make – negative on occasion, or positive, as the case may be. And this possesses far more power than do passive reflections of the factual world. Why not confess as much and begin living from the inside out? Why go on pretending to be 'objective' or merely rational, when that is not our real nature at all? The natural thing for a human being is response and creation, not standing back. That much at least I learned from the mad agonies I suffered in boyhood – and from the trees.

Nightwatchmen

This moment, this being, is the thing. My life is all life in little. The moon, the planets, pass around my heart. The sun, now hidden by the round bulk of this earth, shines into me, and in me as well. The gods and the angels both good and bad are like the hairs of my own head, seemingly numberless, and growing from within. I people the cosmos from myself, it seems, yet what am I? A puff of dust, or a brief coughing spell, with emptiness and silence to follow.

Wait now. If all past time really were vanished and gone, that would indeed turn true of me as well. Again, if future time were not yet come, then I am a skeleton in labour with a stone. But is the human view of past, present and future accurate at all?

Saint Augustine, for one, said no. In logic, he maintained, time has to be conceived as a cohesive and continual present, an eternal Now. All things pass by us, or we pass by them, an old Greek poet said, but this is an illusion brought about by some strange astigmatism in human consciousness. Medieval Meister Eckhart of the Rhineland reached the same conclusion as Saint Augustine. Like a man peering down into a rain-barrel he was, until one day the bottom fell out for him, whereupon he knew his mind was not really the barrel; it was the well, or Mind in general, or the Godhead, which re-creates all things from boundless nothingness, in play, at every moment of the night and day. When the time came for him to return into the boundless, Eckhart promised, he would not even have been missed. Why so? Because he would never have been away but in the Godhead's play . . .

A person went out walking in a city late at night. There seemed to be no one about. He heard no sound but that of his own footsteps. Streetlamps were dim and few. There was no traffic even on the distant avenues. The sky was overcast, like darkly gleaming iron. He kept on walking. He was passing a vacant lot when somebody jumped out at him. Where was he going? That seemed to be the question, toothlessly mumbled in a strange language. He admitted he did not know.

'Lucky you!' said the old fellow, in English, clearly now. 'Me, I'm a nightwatchman. I've got my shack, behind the fence, and crickets, believe it or not! Good night. Go home and get some sleep.'

The cricket only sings of love; the firefly burns with it, according to a Japanese poet. Imprison a firefly between your hands; his light glimmers through your fingers. What light is that? A jittery old nightwatchman's lamp, shining through the cracks in a fence around a vacant lot . . .

'Prior to creatures, in the eternal Now, I have played before the Father in an eternal stillness.' Meister Eckhart's words, more or less.

Short Pants

Vision and Chaos – that shapeless but highly respectable divine couple – were upset. His Serene Majesty, the Monarch of the World, made no mistakes at all, so far as they could discover. The King's measures were forthright and scrupulously correct at every turn. This made Vision see red, and Chaos churn within. So they produced a son, an ugly but cheery little dwarf, who grew up in extreme poverty on the earth.

When he had come of age, the dwarf sought and received an audience with the King. 'I am the person of least account in all your Majesty's domains,' the dwarf complained. 'My lot would be much easier to bear if I had property, at least. All I ask is this. Grant me as much of your kingdom as I can cover in a hop, skip and jump!' The Monarch, smiling indulgently, agreed to do so.

The dwarf's hop swept like flame from pole to pole of the planet. His skip ranged like lightning around the upper air. A final jump, and he was gone beyond the sun. Thus children vanish into age. Yet they return, generation by generation, to claim their patrimony from the Monarch of the World . . .

Sometimes in infancy, before I fell asleep, processions would form up in the abyss beyond my nursery bed. They used to wind into view over my feet, my knees, and carefully motionless hands. Goblins, elf-ladies, troupes of gnomes, animals, knights, acrobats and musicians came to me. But if I were to invite any particular diversion, the whole lot vanished instantly. Nor would those particular beings ever return. Crepuscular creatures, they were. And they knew me; they saw that I was there. Now and again a clown might kick his crimson heels high in the air or a Crusader dipped his spear as a signal, before passing down and away. They came as shy friends, not as imaginings. No longer may I witness them, yet sometimes even to this day I glimpse their colour campfires at the bottom of the stream of ordinary vision.

A trap-door opened in the ceiling right over my crib, upon a time. An angel came down with a ladder, to fetch me. She brought me up through the trap-door into an ancient Egyptian chamber, where rows of Pharaohs sat enthroned. And one by one, courteously, without a word, each Pharaoh greeted me. Each one of those Pharaohs leaned forward to acknowledge my coming with due solemnity. Later, the angel led me down into my crib again . . . Now, if that dream was mere 'wish-fulfilment' as the saying goes, then babies have rather astonishing wishes.

Sunt geminae somni portae, Virgil explained. There are two gates of sleep. The first gate, built of gleaming ivory, stands wide open to falsity. That gate, of course, commands a busy thoroughfare. But elsewhere stands a second gate of a secret and narrow kind, made of two curving horns, and it permits easy passage to true spirits alone.

Regard someone sleeping. Look well, because that person may be a small child again, dancing once more upon the knees of the mountains . . .

At five years old, I waved ancient comrades off to school. My mother said I was not old enough to go with them as yet. 'You'll learn your letters all too soon,' she confided. 'For one more year, I want you to study things as they are.' Puzzled, I disengaged my hand, and Mother stepped back into the house. Alone I wandered in the opposite direction from the one which my comrades had taken. Mrs Amory cackled warningly from her rocker on her yellow porch. She was over ninety. I waved to her, and strolled on. Mr Kiley's stable came next. It held a broken-down hansom cab upon which my friends and I had often played. Beyond the stable was a weed-grown lot where Mr Kiley's horses long ago had grazed. I walked in slow motion, and guessed I must be a good mile from home. By adult reckoning, no doubt, I had gone half a block. It had rained in the night, but now the sky was clearing. A Y-shaped stick fell dark and wet into my hand. Perhaps I tore it from a tree, but my recollection is that it simply fell to me. Then I found myself squatting by a sidewalk puddle as the clouds parted down below. The magic wand which I held seemed to dip into the water of its own accord. I watched it writing blue and silver letters upside-down.

The next memory that comes back to me concerns a puppet theatre and the sound of trolls rolling their bowls under Thunder Mountain. Rip Van Winkle, I understood, had grown up to be a puppet. But now the lullaby of a shrill cataract sank Rip in century-long sleep. Meanwhile a dragon sprang at me personally through that tin-and-tinsel waterfall. The dragon's wings were the glittering white implacable irreversible torrent of every moment . . .

My mother told a story once about a little girl in school, a foreign child who found it hard to understand just what was going on. Her seeming stupidity so irritated the teacher that finally he clapped a tall paper cone of a dunce-cap on her curly head, sternly bidding her stand in the corner with her back to the class and be still. More baffled than embarrassed by his abuse, she did so, wondering why the whole class meanwhile hissed and bubbled with contemptuous laughter. In fact she rather liked facing the wall and standing very still. The dunce-cap she wore seemed more like a sorcerer's cap to her. Slowly the scornful laughter faded from her ears, to be replaced by true happy laughter. She found herself in school in the Clear Land, playing a standing-still game with her earthly friends – all of them now transformed and lifted up into their breezy, balmy-natured selves. She played well too, for she was very still, that little foreigner. And when at last the earthly teacher released her from the bondage of the corner, she turned to face the actual class with a smile of perfect happiness.

Did something of that sort occur in Mother's own child-hood? She developed slowly, was often ill, and considered a dullard at school, for the genius in her shunned exposure.

The Pure Land, the Clear Land . . .

The Garden of Eden they condemn, plough under, and roll smooth. School makes a dusty drill-ground of your soul, and later on a chicken-run. 'I came! I saw! I conquered!' Every day, and all about, that same glad shout. All up and down the pecking order it rings out. But who is being conquered? Children, for a start.

When I was nine or thereabouts, my whole family, grand-parents and all, got into a huge open touring-car and drove away. Smiling and waving they left me alone, and at the same time darkness fell. I turned back to the house in the gloom. I climbed the steps of the front porch and stood there wondering. Everyone had gone, and yet the house did not feel empty after all. As I thought this, my clothes fell away. Wondering what to do, I noticed a gleaming white garment neatly folded over the porch railing. I slipped it on; the front door swung open at the same time – not outward but inward.

The rest I can remember only in a glimmering sort of way. I was welcomed in onto a mountain platform of living rock, and asked to gaze upon the pure dawn of the world. Yes, I saw it.

My father woke me up early that morning; he had promised to take me out into the woods to glimpse some rare bird or other.

'I was dreaming', I told him, 'of colours which are not on earth.'

He smiled indulgently: 'Describe them to me.'

At once I realized the impossibility, while with my inner eye I watched those colours disappear. Of course they are here still, although they cannot be perceived by physical eyes, nor in the memory. Those colours precede body and mind alike. They are the green and not green shoots of everlastingness. They are the blue not blue dawn boy, the yellow not yellow dawn boy, the white not white dawn boy, and finally father sun . . .

It must have been at age eleven or so that I was given the part of an old Viking bard in a school play. We had a warrior feast right on stage, where they served real gingerbread pro-vided by some doting parent. Greedily, I stuffed my cheeks with all the gingerbread I could get. And then, a moment later as it seemed to me, I heard my chieftain's loud command to rise and entertain the throng. Rising to stand, masked in my ether-stinking beard, with harp in hand I bowed; and swallowed, but the sticky mess between my teeth would not go down. So, thinking hard, I plucked a chord; the silent audience stared. Doubtless a Viking would have spat his gingerbread straight out, but I dared not do that. Instead, I plucked a second chord, and thickly I declaimed –

'Friends, fellow-warriors, harken to my joyful song!'

No one rushed to stop me from going on. I plucked a third chord and began some gingerbread jumble of joyful tongue, some big mumble. And that's the story of my life.

J.

The first separation of the sexes, and with this the first marriage, occurred because the Serpent cast a veil over Adam and across every sense that was in him, except one. Namely, the Thought of Light, who hid herself away in Adam's heart. Adam thought nothing, felt nothing, yet in his dream he willed to bring the Thought of Light forth from his own rib. But the Thought of Light is unattainable, and although Adam pursued her in his dream he could not seize her. Then she took pity upon him, and came out, and arose before him in female form. Immediately his drunken sleep departed. Adam became sober from the intoxication of the darkness surrounding the Thought of Light. Then she removed the veil from about him, and Adam recognized his own essence in her and said:

'This is now bone of my bones, and flesh of my flesh.'

Is that how it began? The legend brings J. home again from far-off Hawaii (where she is on holiday with the children now) into my mind's eye.

Yet having a mind's eye is just what makes human beings stand back and look upon things as a passing show, rather than directly engaging in reality. Hence we become detached from the animals, from our friends, and finally even from our own simplest and happiest instincts. Next comes quarrelling, and war, and history, the nightmare from which Man cannot awaken. Is this the pattern? Is Man from the beginning doomed by his gift of inward vision?

I was feeling fretful this morning when I crossed the footbridge to the serpent shrine. Watching a pair of ducks paddle and feed in the brown shadow of the bridge, I forgot my problem, whatever it may have been. They were amber in colour, those two, gleaming and turning round and round on the surface of darker brown. And they seemed happily married, so peaceful. But then, stooping his neck with a swift snakelike motion, the male parted his bill a bit to nip the downy region in under his partner's tail. She gave a faint shriek of a quack, and then a small shiver, as he released her.

Maybe the best that bird or beast or person can hope to achieve in these sour times is harmony through conflict. Continuous conflict, of course, the problem being to create continuous harmony as well. *Zazen* helps me, a little, to do so. It helps thousands of other Americans too. Even my home town has a Zen community now. Hundreds of Zen-Buddhist priests and nuns are practising at this moment in the United States. And yet a Kyoto roshi has said that Americans are like translucent ants, wallowing in a sugar-bowl.

True or false? Most American followers of Zen emphasize physical discipline as against study. This may be a healthy reaction to the literary and aesthetic approach of past decades. One should pursue occult learning in the light of day, and luminous meditation in the dark of night, so Isshu Miura taught. That way, he explained, nature vitalizes learning at the same time that learning deepens nature. Masao Abe put the same point this way: 'Too much study makes Zen too thin; too much practice makes it too thick.'

If *zazen* were all that was needed to attain *satori*, 'frogs would be Buddhas,' so they say.

One Saturday evening at Myoshinji, early on, J. seemed in a mud-coloured mood of anger and melancholy. My own attitude, in *zazen*, was not so bad for a change. I felt fairly calm, but for the sense of J.'s misery which kept agitating the surface of my thoughts. It was then that she lifted her hands, palms together in an attitude of prayer, to request a beating with the *keisaku*. I knew at once that she was doing so; I saw what happened, not really, but from the corner of the corner of my unblinking left eye. Abe-sensei stopped in front of her, and bowed. She bent down from the hips, while remaining in the lotus position, until her shoulders nearly touched the floor. Abe struck hard, on her right shoulder-blade, and paused, then struck again, hard. My legs were locked in place; I sat more still, if anything, than before. Again the *keisaku* whistled and fell, across her left shoulder-blade now, with a furious crack, and yet again it descended on the same spot. The terrific shock of it, rather than pain, was what my own anxiously roving nerve-ends picked up. I sat stunned, as if a sheet of electricity had flicked across my back. Rage rose in me, but it was altogether impersonal, a fiery heat, reasonless, from within. The hair at the back of my neck bristled; I could feel it. Abe-sensei was bowing now to J., his effort made, and she was returning his bow, low to the floor; she could still bend her back, it seemed. Shouldering his *keisaku* once more, Abe-sensei passed slowly on down the line, in front of me. To leap up from a *zazen* position is not physically possible, for one must first unfold one's legs in order to do so. There was the instinct to leap up, the utterly unthinking animal surge of rage which I felt, but fortunately I could not. I sat like a rock, more rigid than ever before or since in my whole life. And then slowly came peacefulness. It came from J. That she was fine now my heart knew. Although at a distance from each other, and motionless, we were joining hands. It was like the beginnings of my boyhood dreams. Hand in hand, we were passing now through the paper wall of Abe-sensei's schoolroom, and that good man smiled to see us go.

Now, here is a mystery. Throughout the entire proceeding I had not for one moment ceased to pray. *Nāmu Āmidā Bu-*, *Nāmu Āmidā Bu-*, I kept on repeating. 'Glory to the Lord of Light.' And then it was as if that primal Buddha brought me and J. together for a time, in his Pure Land. Yes, we were there together, not caring whether such a being or such a place 'actually' exists or not.

Abe-sensei himself would almost certainly disapprove, if he but knew, my secret practice of silently and prayerfully invoking Amida Buddha throughout the *zazen* sessions which he directs.

He does all he can to preserve and propagate the pure Zen traditions which Dogen brought from China to Japan, and Dogen adamantly taught that sitting and hitting suffice. *Zazen* ought not to be practised in conjunction with any other observances, in short. But both 'ought' and 'ought not' are dirty words from my viewpoint, and moreover I find prayer helps a lot – even when I do not know to whom or to what I presume to pray. J., however, does something else in *zazen*, something known only to herself. But of course we are not alone, never alone. A priest of Korean Rinzai told me the other day that in his sect the combining of *zazen* with invocation of Amida Buddha is standard. J.'s secret way of meditation, too, is probably commonplace in some part of the world, since human beings everywhere share one and the same sacredness, whether it be described as Buddha-nature, or the Christ, or something else.

Every church must strive, by its man-bound nature, to maintain preponderance in the heart of man. But if all of us men, women and children were to really obey Christ's command – 'That ye love one another' – then every church would soon wither away for lack of things to do. Why so? Because then our true church and temple would soon prove to be each person's home. It is actually true now in fact, although this goes unrecognized. Hence we defile ourselves, with marital quarrelling and so on, far more severely than we know. Domestic strife occurs precisely where heaven ought to open, that is to say in the innermost circle of hell, an iceboundness insoluble, and mystery absolute. I speak now of my own altar . . .

Our children chose us to be theirs, way back in the void somewhere, and this we know. We played together, all of us, in the stillness of the eternal Now. For these reasons, and not because of any virtue that I possess, family life has been fabulously blessed in my case. All the more so because J. understands these things much better than I do. And yet, despite all this, we have defiled our house with quarrelling, and doubtless will again. But how is such abomination possible? After a desperate two-day struggle with J. over nothing at all some weeks ago, I seated myself in a hotel room, in my best approximation of the physical posture recommended for *zazen* meditation, and earnestly addressed myself to this general question. An unconsciously comic and pathetic scene it must have been, though no one witnessed it; and no useful response, naturally, arose within my thought. Finally, I fell asleep sitting up . . .

In my dream, I dared to ask again, whereupon it seemed that I was taken up and effortlessly transported to a barren height, and there some imageless being instructed me, without words but along the following lines:

'Greedy passion is the reason. You creatures were created for the purpose of incarnating and giving form to heavenly energies, hence your hunger, thirst and suffering never cease. As to the purpose of all this, it is unknown on earth, even in the accomplishment, nor do non-physical beings know it. Yet to such beings, of whom I am one, human suffering seems a marvellous and rare privilege, devoutly to be lived through. There is no other way for you.'

Should I accept the solemn purport of this dream, or not? Some would say that a demon counselled me. Others would laugh the whole thing off with the comment that I must indeed have been depressed at the time. Pious Buddhists, on the contrary, would almost certainly point out the fact that Sakyamuni taught the same thing as my dream. Human suffering stems from thirsty craving, and nothing else. The Sutras almost uniformly insist on that point, at least. To associate thirsty craving with J., however, is like putting darkness together with a lamp, or heaviness with a flower. As for myself, I have been young and harrowed by unquenchable desires, but such no longer seem central to me. So then, what is my conclusion?

'If you ask me,' Saint Augustine said with regard to some metaphysical query, 'I do not know. But when you do not ask, then I know.' Similarly when the doctor asks if something hurts, it may not.

Athos

Zen lore is stuffed with lessons about how this or that monk, way back in T'ang China, 'received enlightenment' when his superior tweaked his nose, or kicked him in the belly, or whatever. Distance appears to lend a saving dignity to these stories. To me they sound funny, as often as not. Yet I incline to believe such tales. Why? Because experience has taught me that it is possible to enter a holy place, even today, and receive from some authority there a sudden illumination. In my own case, however, this did not occur at a Zen-Buddhist monastery but on Mount Athos. I cannot in good conscience describe such experience as truly 'enlightening' in my case; but it would have been so, doubtless, had I myself been ready to accept enlightenment. There was the hermit Simon, first. I mentioned him before somewhere in these pages. Then later on there was a telepathic monk, believe it or not, and finally an abbot who transmitted wisdom by gesture alone. But first I had better describe the place itself:

Athos is a mountainous peninsula in the northern Aegean sea. The peninsula measures forty miles or so from its narrow neck in the north down to the triple peak at its tip. This peak rises bare and sheer from forested foothills to a great height. It looks transparent, in a way. Both by night and by day, the Holy Mountain shines like a fountain of cliff and pasture, mist and crystal, earth and air. It is a wilderness, by and large, even today. Mount Athos has a meagre history, but strange as well. Many have felt its pull . . .

Some twenty-four centuries ago, a prince named Alexarchus founded what he hoped would be a pure utopia upon Athos. He taught his subjects to regard themselves as 'Uranidae' – Sons of Heaven – and furthermore to speak a language of his own invention. The project failed, and the first Uranidae vanished utterly. Their only relic was a statue of Apollo standing by the shore at the base of the Holy Mountain. It remained until, according to legend, the Virgin Mary stepped ashore at Athos. Then Apollo's statue shattered into fragments. Mary blessed the Mountain. Also, if this can be credited, she commanded it to receive no women ever again. Another thousand years, more or less, passed while the Mountain slept. Finally, in the summer of 965, a Byzantine ship was becalmed off its southernmost promontory. One of the sailors cried out that Athos called to him. He swam ashore to take up residence by himself in a cave. The ship sailed on as if released.

In the millennium since Athos claimed its first hermit, flocks of spiritual seekers have followed him to the Mountain. Athos has twenty monasteries now, all dating back to medieval times. They look like castles, bristling from the heights and the sea-cliffs. No brave show of pennants tops the towers, but gilt crosses glitter there. Inside the massive gates are beehive cells, great libraries, cloisters, and churches. Icons glow secretly within, like gems in a cavern. Sometimes you come upon a vast fresco filled with black skies and gleaming, lilting landscapes and swart, silver-bearded, God-possessed figures.

The paintings by Panselinos, for instance, at the Prototon of Karyes, surpass even El Greco. I would have spent the day in their presence, had not some churlish monks resented my standing about. They seemed to think that I would fade the frescoes simply by staring. We argued the point. Finally the monks tossed me out. That was a shock. I crawled off, as it were, in a fury. It struck me then for the first time, and poignantly, that not one high song could be heard along the Mountain's flank. No children's cries flashed anywhere, and no laughter. The weirdest thing about Athos is the Virgin's supposed prohibition. No women and hence no families are allowed. Not one.

A second prohibition, in force on Athos now, bars Russian novitiates. The Greek Orthodox authorities – churchmen who rule the Holy Mountain – say they must guard against 'Communist infiltration'. Therefore, what used to be the largest monastery on Athos is crumbling. Panteleimonos, where the Russians always used to come, now numbers just a few old men who arrived there before the First World War. Like dried leaves, these ragged monks move scrapily about their sagging corridors. They are no longer used to seeing visitors. But one plucked at my wrist and drew me in to his poor cell to show me something. It proved to be a fresco of a saint feeding a sandwich to a wild bear.

Panteleimonos possesses a graveyard levelled back into the mountainside. There are many headstones here. Their inscriptions speak for persons buried centuries ago. Over the graveyard stands a single, unbelievably enormous, cypress tree. Its roots, plainly, grope down among the ancient dead. The tall, tall trunk and prayerfully close-clustered branches of this tree bring the dead up again, into the fiery air. The shadow of the cypress points downhill across the gaily glittering onion domes of the decayed monastery. That shadow makes one think of a sundial. Or of a wheel which is half-buried and yet turning still . . .

One evening on Athos I found myself at table with an Athenian playboy and a cynical French journalist. A monk joined us without a word, as if he had been expected. The conversation turned to the names of the monasteries on the Holy Mountain. The Athenian said he could remember only two or three. 'Recite those,' the monk suggested. 'The rest will come to you!'

'Karyes, Lavros . . .'

'One. Two,' the monk said. 'Yes. Go on, and I'll keep count.' And thereupon the youth proceeded through the entire list of twenty with no further hitch.

I looked hard at the monk for the first time. His forehead was bulbous, deeply indented at the temples. His eyes – deep-set under the shadow of his brow – glittered as if with interior light. His nose was high and narrow. His wide cheekbones were slanted like a Slav's. His mouth was thin and firm. His long squared-off beard was the colour of iron. His robe had once been black but age had weathered it to a warm brownish green. His finger-nails were dirty and broken. His hands were large, calloused like a sailor's. He touched no food, I noticed. Was he real, or just a ghost? Real, I decided, since my companions seemed to accept him with equanimity. But had this mysterious stranger projected the names of all the monasteries into the Athenian's mind?

The journalist put some questions in Greek. How many persons were there in the monk's own community?

'*Dekaepta*,' the monk said, brusquely. 'Seventeen.'

'That's quite a few!'

'Many or not, it's seventeen.'

That answer seemed as down to earth and as direct as it had been quick. I relaxed somewhat. Just then the monk looked full at me and put one finger to his lips. The gesture seemed to be a warning of some kind. And then, without a word, he spoke inside my mind. It took me a moment to realize that this was silent speech. Nobody else had noticed anything.

'Shall we talk this way?' the monk had asked.

I doubted my senses. I was afraid as well, naturally. No one had ever stepped inside my mind before, so far as I had been aware. Instinct told me to play dumb this time. I pushed a pack of cigarettes towards the monk. He set it aside. I offered him a plate of cherries. He refused this by tilting back his head. I filled his glass and my own with wine. Resignedly, he drank with me. I put my glass down hard. Lightly, silently, the monk returned his own empty glass to the table. 'Listen,' he insisted, inside my mind. So I listened.

'Your friend whom I helped a moment ago reminds me of Jesus.'

'That', I thought, 'is ridiculous. The two have nothing whatsoever in common.'

'Jesus was young and brave. So is this boy ready to die.'

The monk himself, I felt certain, was very old indeed. He seemed to be composed of hair, eyes, skin, sinew and bone. There was nothing so yielding and moist as flesh itself about this man.

'All of us are deathward bound,' I thought. 'Herded together in the dark.'

Instantly, the monk set me straight. Still in my head, he said: 'That's not correct. People are in the light but they themselves radiate darkness by their thoughts. Look at your friends and see the light press in around them; how lovely it is. Watch how darkness and blindness ooze from their heads, like smoke, to mingle with the light.'

I saw what he meant. I seemed to see all that with my physical eyes.

The silent thrust of his mind, now withdrawn, left me dazzled. Think how bewildered an ancient Greek would have been if someone had shown him television. I was that baffled by the monk's deliberate telepathy. And now a curious, faint familiar smell came to me. Puzzled, I sniffed the air. I remembered far, far back as I did so. This was my father's smell as I knew it in infancy, when I used to crawl in with him at dawn.

'You may stay and study with me.'

'Thank you. There are people on Corfu whom I love and who need me. There is an art to which I feel dedicated. And finally, my appetites – '

'I know,' he interrupted silently. 'You should practise.' With that enigmatic suggestion the monk rose, smiling grimly. He stepped away. I felt a sort of pang. But he had only gone to fetch a toothpick, and now he came back. 'Like this,' the monk explained, still in my mind. He sat down and began to pick his teeth. 'If you cannot yet quite control your appetites you will at least be cleanly about them. And when you return to the world remember to set your glass down gently. That will be a sign.'

'Words', I thought, 'are my kind of sign.'

'Do not suppose that we have spoken here in words. Our souls have walked together; that is all. The day may come when you can walk alone, or seemingly alone. Remember me.'

Dinner was over. We all four got up from the table. The monk turned to leave. I stooped to kiss his hand, but he was too quick for me; he made his arm rigid. '*Ochi!*' he said aloud. The word means 'No', and it was the only word he actually spoke to me. I straightened to look at him for the last time. I meant to ask his name, but he had moved away. A moment later he was gone. No one had any idea who he might have been . . .

Dionysius was a Christian saint, yet the Greek peasantry credit him with having invented wine. They may confuse him with the ancient god of wine Bacchus, who was also known as Dionysus (without the second 'i'). In any case, the most hospitable monastery which I found on Athos was the one dedicated to Saint Dionysius.

Whether by coincidence or not, the monks of that place cultivate their own vineyard to produce a very dark strong wine. Down in the cavernous refectory, one afternoon, they plied me with wine by the tumbler until I had some trouble standing up. Afterwards they took me upstairs to see some frescoes of the Last Judgment, which dated from the fourteenth century. These frescoes seemed to be filled with falling fire-bombs.

The monks asked if I understood the meaning of the pictures. I shook my head uncertainly. Fire is one great purifier; wine is another. Euripides wrote of 'orgies in the mountains, with holy purifications'. Servius Honoratus, the Roman antiquarian, states that the rites of Bacchus were for the purification of souls.

I was absently gnawing a cucumber, I recall, when word came that the abbot wished to entertain me on his balcony. His name was Theodosius. His tiny balcony commanded an enormous and unbroken stretch of plum-coloured sea. He and I sat knee to knee, sipping still more wine and looking down with joy over the waves below. I felt as soaring birds must feel, at home up there. Theodosius beamed approvingly. His eyes were brilliant brown, his face ruddy, his beard black as the wine. He spoke like a brother to me and asked me something very directly. My Greek is minimal; moreover I was high. Apologetically, I confessed that I failed to follow his question. He smiled, as if delighted, and gestured with his glass. The sun and wine mixed in his plump brown hand. His black sleeve brushed the horizon line. It was as if he had opened a thin venetian blind of the transparent air, and let it drop again. The abbot nodded meaningfully . . .

Drink up, and at the bottom of your wine glass you may find a little sediment. It is the 'mother of the wine'. Mother and matter are related words, of course. When you drink, you are swallowing both of your parents: matter mixed with the void. Yet your experience is single. The taste of the wine, for example, cannot be separated out from the liquid itself. As with wine, so with the whole world. The world splits nowhere. That is what the abbot showed me from his balcony, with a gesture only.

The world is not twice or more, but once.

I'd better pause on this point for a minute. There is very little that I know for sure, but this I do know. Why? Because Theodosius showed it to my soul's perception; it is not something out of a book. However, as I was much later to learn, Dr Erwin Schrodinger's Cambridge lectures on mind and matter reached the same conclusion. Besides, this truth forms the core of the 'Dionysian' tradition in Greek Christian thought. Eleven years after getting that merciful flash of light from the abbot, I came upon the following summation of the Dionysian attitude in Rudolph Steiner's *Riddles of Philosophy*: 'When the soul liberates itself from everything that it can perceive and think as *being*, when it also transcends beyond what it is capable of thinking as *non-being*, then it can spiritually divine the realm of *over-being*, the hidden godhead.'

Sci-Fi

The stars above, in their billions, appear to pour out fire without stint, and receive no discernible return of it. The case of our own sun is typical, and it seems terribly wasteful. Earth and the other planets drink only a sip from the oceans of light and heat which our sun sends forth every moment. No wonder, then, that scientists predict the inevitable winding down and freezing of the entire universe – a cold dark cinder world at last. Are they right about this? The Hindus do not believe so. They say that their Saviour – 'Vishnu the Preserver' – sacrifices himself to the sun as a sort of food.

Yesterday evening I walked out beyond Shugakuin, and there I encountered an enigmatic figure in a field. The light of the setting sun rayed in under the brim of his straw hat. Having been crucified and exalted, he ignored that. As I came near, sparrows flew up from the furrow at his buried foot. Whirling away over the hill, they quickly fell from sight again. Now I stood close enough to shake hands with him, if such a thing were possible. He had no hands, however, nor a face either, nor flesh, nor bone. Some farmer had created him in the farmer's own image, ancient since birth, of sticks and straw and a few rags and an old broom. Mud clogged the creases of his clothes.

Bodhidharma, the First Patriarch of Zen, is said to have collapsed seven times and arisen eight times when he received enlightenment. This scarecrow, too, must often have fallen, as children do . . .

In the English newspaper which an acquaintance left with me, a forward-looking space-technician points out that astronauts who die far from home may prove embarrassing. One could dispose of their bodies through an air-lock, but in that case the corpses would continue to accompany the vehicle. 'The other travellers might be distressed', the scientist observes, 'to see Harry and Joe keeping up after all.' His solution: backpack jets, designed to shoot dead astronauts into the solar field of gravity. Columbus dumped his deceased comrades into the ocean; why shouldn't future space-captains dip their dead straight into the sun itself? 'Eventually, each one will be incinerated in a blaze of glory!' Translated into factual terms, that means that each body disposed of in such a manner will become a part of the sun's own fire. Therefore not a single atom of Harry and Joe can possibly remain human, not even in theory. But this is a sobering thought, and somehow paradoxical.

Democritus – the ancient Greek who has been called the father of modern physics – put our dilemma in a nutshell. 'Man', said Democritus, 'must recognize that he is far removed from how things actually are.' That might be something for a space-captain to recite, as he jettisons deceased companions into the blazing sun.

'Nothing exists but atoms and the void.' So said Democritus.

But when the philosopher reached that decision – momentous for science – were his eyes open, or closed? Even in deep darkness, photons swarm before our eyes, exiguous yet energetic sparks which occasionally mass into actual images. The atom-void duality appears less clear to modern heirs of Democritus, in any case, than it was to himself. In cyclotrons, atoms play into nothingness, as it were, and the reverse also seems to occur. A Rinzai roshi has been known to shout: 'Nothing is energy!'

Nothing is energy, inside and out. The proposition seems to make no sense and yet experience – *zazen*, for instance, or fasting, or prayer – lends it support. No self has ever lived except in relation to not-self. People appear and vanish again like freckles on the bright sleek epidermis of emptiness . . .

Relaxing in a Tokyo club, the other night, a Japanese author tried to set me straight on literature. 'Right now', he remarked, 'some old lady may be out gathering medicinal herbs on Mount Fuji; by the magic light of the moon, while her grandson analyzes rocks brought down from the moon itself. In other words, the past and the future collide for us. Time is being folded up like a fan. The question is, how should writers respond to this new situation? It may be that the old-fashioned novel, with its leisurely time-sense and creaking machinery of coincidence, must go. Non-fiction also is suspect, because of its equally out-of-date linear logic. What we need now is a brand-new literature designed for the crowds of people hurtling through our rush-hour age. In short: science-fiction. Ever tried it?'

'No,' I said, 'but I have been tempted by mythology. The Greek god Zeus chained the clever Titan Prometheus to a Caucasian peak. Thereafter, for about a thousand years until the building of Galileo's telescope, science slept. But Zeus vanished long ago and finally Prometheus gained his freedom again. Our streets are trembling, at this moment, beneath the tread of the invisible and all-too-generous Titan.'

'Well,' said the author, 'even if there's some truth in that, what can we do about it? Prometheus is not about to be put down again. Besides, he builds far more than he destroys.'

Right, I thought. In the Ginza, and out along the water-front, at airports, and in the industrial suburbs, new monuments to the Titan arise. Their anodized-aluminium and glass out-gleams the gold-sheathed obelisks which Queen Hatshepsut conjured up three and a half thousand years ago. Their canti-levered terraces recall on a much grander scale the Hanging Gardens of Babylon. The Titan's hardhat armies swarm clanking across the continents, and his oil gushers outhiss the Basilisk. His skyscrapers stand mean as the blind wink of a sardine can on a garbage dump. His nuclear tests glow beautiful as rubies sunk from the tender pink earlobes of a female poisoner . . .

In summertime, back in New York, the morning glories on my penthouse terrace used to flourish their blue trumpets to the sun. Each day, when I got back from work, the sun would have begun to sink between the rabbit ears of the Majestic Towers across Central Park. The flowers were starting to fold and fade at that point, visibly withering away. In order to forget the day's cares, I helped the vines twine their tendrils around the roof railings. After a time I found that they used to unwind again – as it were behind my back – and reverse all my plans. They had their own manner of growing, after all. So I stopped playing God.

One sunset hour, an old school friend named Alan Harring-ton came to my terrace for a drink. The pale mute withering of the flowers made him wince. 'Death is here too,' he com-plained.

I shrugged: 'What can we do?'

'Plenty! But it requires a crash-programme. Science must produce a pill which will prolong human life indefinitely. Don't laugh. This has to happen in our own lifetimes. Otherwise, what's the use? Don't pretend you're not terrified of death.'

'Tomorrow', I said, 'these vines will be loaded with fresh blossoms. We're not childless, thank God!'

Almost angrily, Alan writhed in his deck-chair: 'God is just an abstraction. Death, however, is real. Death is earnest, and Death wins every single time. Death will take us and our children and our children's children – as Death always has done – unless and until we stand up to Him!'

'Wait,' I said. 'What if the opposite case is being debated now by twins of yours and mine, off in some anti-sunset of their own? What we call death is not their enemy. But what we call birth may be. It's possible that every death in matter means a rebirth over there – in anti-matter. If so, then the reverse is also possible. Every birth in matter may mean death elsewhere. It looks as if the world must breathe molecules like ourselves, inhaling us as matter and exhaling us as anti-matter; something like that.'

Alan had risen, drink in hand, and walked off to the far end of the terrace. Now he flung his drink against the vines. Whirling round, he called out in a choking voice: 'Coward! You treat the whole thing as a game of words!'

'No, I do not. I think what you propose is a revolt of the molecules, to somehow strangle the world's breath. But even if our poor humanity were capable of that, it would be just the opposite of what you want.'

'Oh, well,' he said. 'You needn't shout.'

My teachers seem to draw me ever deeper into the darkness of ignorance, where knowledge flickeringly burns. The more I learn the less I understand. 'A baby is an unlearned saint, and a saint is a learned baby.' So said the Shinto sage Nobuyoshi Watarai. For me, however, there can be no question of saintliness. Just knowledge and ignorance, mixed. Yet one's instructors also require forgiveness. Hence the mutual bowing which precedes and follows *keisaku* discipline in the *zendo* . . .

If one of two organisms were placed in a box and launched through space at almost the speed of light on a long elliptical orbit, it would return unaged. Meanwhile the second organism would have been replaced by sons, grandsons and great-grandsons in turn. Science-minded people agree – don't they? – that this is true. The next Rip Van Winkle will be a space-traveller, they say. But how about mental travel? Thought is instantaneous. How about soul travel? That 'Box' which Einstein posited for his not-yet-performable experiment could be a coffin, after all. The organism or body involved might prove to be the disposable first stage of something unexpected. In short, we ourselves may vanish only to return again, and speedily, to some far-distant era.

Scientists maintain that light is the speediest thing known. All right, but what about spirit? They don't plot that . . .

They say that no two snowflakes, no two thoughts, and no two people are alike. What about that idea? What does it do to the concept of 'scientific objectivity' in general? Perhaps the whole business of some things being 'objective' and others 'subjective' is just untrue. Granting the fact that there has been a great deal of sharp definition and debate expended on this question over the past few hundred years, perhaps it is merely a verbal quibble after all – and, indeed, a misunderstanding.

Ask your heart to discriminate between 'objective' and 'subjective' truths. It will not so discriminate. The heart refuses to distinguish between the two. Or rather, for the heart, such distinctions are like snowflakes on a hot stove. And so, ultimately, are the distinctions between like and dislike. Because, as soon as you begin to notice something in a liking or disliking way, it has gone already. Only when you fail to notice, fail to discriminate, and yet pay full attention at the same time – only when you achieve a state of alert emptiness, in other words – does anything worthwhile occur subjectively. Good things happen when you are courteous to them, to the events themselves.

Once in a temple garden at Daitokuji, I listened to a twig broom being wielded steadily by a shabby old man in a green grove – green with the ageless, seemingly ever-young plants which were first to grow and multiply upon the earth, with lichen and with moss. The old man was sweeping the green floor clean of crimson maple leaves. He drove a wave-shaped drift of leaves before him without pause, never even pausing to shift his broom except when he turned at the far end of the wave, and again at the near end. The pauseless hustling of the leaves, bracketed by those turns at roughly three- or four-minute intervals, was soothing. He seemed a master of the broom, and of much more than that; his sweeping was a kind of meditation which I shared. And then I saw, not far above his head, a single maple leaf unfallen. It trembled like a spark upon a spider-thread. In the whole shadowy grove only this one leaf still remained aloft. It seemed to breathe towards me, in sympathy. And why? Had I ever seen such a thing before? Yes, in the womb.

Satori happens every day. The only difficult thing is to be aware, to be there as it were . . .

When I was living in a fishing village on the Greek island of Corfu, a yellow-eyed friend whom I shall call Jones appeared out of the blue. He had flown over from New York. Drugs were much on his mind. 'Where do you get yours,' he asked almost at once, snapping his fingers. Vaguely, I gestured towards Albania across the bay. The sun had set. The peaks were shining in the afterglow like strawberry ice-cream. Jones lifted his eyebrows slightly: 'I thought Albania was forbidden territory.'

'So is the drug scene, so far as I'm concerned. I take my trips in imagination alone, here under this arthritic old olive tree.'

Bluntly Jones said: 'I can beat that.'

I handed him an olive. He munched it, made a grimace of disgust, and spat it out upon the ground. 'I brought a tape recording of myself,' he told me, 'under the influence of LSD. I'll play it for you if you like; that will give us something to talk about.'

Dusk had fallen. I brought out wine. A few villagers gathered to sip and listen in on Jones' tape machine, under the olive tree.

'Shit!' cried the tape in the shadows. 'Shit! Shit!' Jones, squatting, twiddled with the knobs. He seemed half entranced by his own monotonous cries. Bogtho the fisher boy attended him like an acolyte. Athena, however, frowned. She was the natural singer in our village and probably she found the tape unmusical. The baker's daughter, Aphrodite, had picked up a few words of English from American sailors. Laughingly, she rolled her eyes at me. Eleutheria sensed something wrong in what was going on. So did little Leonidas, who kept fingering his fly. Joachim was my landlord and the leading figure in our group. He jerked his thumb at the machine and asked: 'What does it say? I keep hearing the same chorus, don't I?'

'Oh, shit!' the machine cried once more.

'It's an expression', I explained, 'from the Egyptian Book of the Dead.'

With that, the machine spun its shrill tripes to a halt. Ephemeral commas lit the deep twilight. Vibrantly they danced, around our tree. Just one or two, then quite a few, then hundreds and finally thousands of fireflies were flashing here and there and everywhere, as far as the eye could see. Athena began singing a lament by Hadzidakis called *The Kiss*, and Joachim joined in.

Thereupon a seeming miracle occurred: the fireflies picked up the rhythm of the song. Increasingly they flashed in unison, as if on cue, until their myriads sparkled as one and the whole evening pulsed like a single heart.

In Sanskrit texts, the word *trisna* is used to indicate primal desire and the endless individuation which springs from the same. The fireflies seemed to signal, repeatedly, the prism-flash of *trisna* itself. Like a prism, the whole power and principle of creation appears passive. Yet it can neither be evaded nor defined. Only because *it* feels like thinking, for example, do I think at all. The sun, too, shines not in and of itself but only through the operation of primal desire.

Pan

My swift dalmatian hound, in the old days, heard things to which I was quite deaf. The dry slither of a coiling adder, perhaps, or nothing physical. Although a brave dog through and through, he used to tremble and shake at such times, and press his shoulder to my knees, to warn me against going on. That often happened on Mount Pendeli, where he was much wiser than I. He made me feel, as I stood still among the scarred marble boulders and scumbled thyme in the heat of the sun, that the ancient pagan deity might be somewhere near at hand. Yes, during those years too, I was indeed afraid of what I failed to understand. I feared to hear Pan's shout along the mountain slope. But not yet, being ignorant, in the street.

'Pan, great Pan is dead!' So certain disappointed pagans proclaimed long ago. Early Christians took up the cry and repeated it with malicious delight. But the very word of his name signifies all and everything, which, if it were to perish, would inevitably be born again at one and the same instant of earthly time.

And even today there are peasants up and down the Balkan peninsula who live in dread that he will shout at them out of a grove, or barn, or by the well, some still evening. Not to mention the thousands upon thousands of urban madmen and madwomen who sit at this moment in mental hospitals with their hands tightly pressed against their ears. The god's name is unfamiliar to most of them, but not terror of him.

Attention is attention, whether Western or Eastern, and it gives life. But inattention destroys us after all. So signifies Pan's maddening shout. Whether willingly or not we lose ourselves in thought. Our brains burn up from within, emitting iron bursts of blasphemy, turning to cinder day by day. Such is the human sacrifice in which everyone must participate.

Early in the fifth century BC, a swift messenger from Athens met the god Pan. It happened when he was running home, across the high mountains of the central Peloponnesus, from an unsuccessful mission to Sparta. Powerful runner that he was, alone and in euphoria, he felt he could outstrip the clouds. Then Pan accosted him, gently. He heard the voice out of a bush of flowers as he ran by. Further along the misty pass he brought himself to a halt, turned, and ran back again to thrust his head in amongst the fragrance whence the voice had come. He saw Pan's heartshaped face, dull gold in the green shade, like a mask hanging there. 'Remind your city to remember me,' the god told him, 'in order that I remember Athens.'

The encounter was deemed worthy of report to the full Assembly of Athenian citizens. They took it seriously, and voted to provide the god with a cave-shrine in the flank of the Acropolis. The reason such a thing had not long since been done was that Athena's city set its face against titanic and irrational forces as a general rule, being dedicated to the goddess of wisdom. But not even that warrior virgin could forever resist Pan's poignant tongue nor the eternal light welling from his dark throat. To visit his shrine even now is still to feel something come like a silent vowel up out of the rock into your feet and knees. If ever Athens falls silent again, he will again be heard. Because Pan, God, is a shout in the street, or just a whispered Word. In the beginning was the Word, of course. If God were to cease speaking the Word, even for one moment, heaven and earth would vanish as a scroll is rolled up. Phenomena do not unfold from each other. Cause and effect are not really in nature but in God. All things return to the Groundless and Boundless, moment by moment, only to be reborn again . . .

Shut your eyes tight and press your fingers to your ears. Wait a bit. Now open your eyes again and take your hands away. How soft, how shadowy, how silent, and yet born anew, everything seems! It is as if you ran your hand along a bamboo stalk. Your fingers reach a joint in the bamboo and briefly hesitate before passing on to another growth or section very like the last – but not the same.

Katsura

A man asked Pai Chang, back in the ninth century, to explain Buddha. 'First, tell me about yourself,' Pai Chang rejoined amiably enough. Readily, the questioner supplied his own name. 'Are you aware', Pai Chang shot back at him, 'of the person whose name you have just given me?' The questioner nodded as if to say he was indeed. Pai Chang thereupon picked up a flywhisk, demanding: 'Do you see what I have here?' Once again the questioner nodded, whereupon Pai Chang turned from him in disgust. Why?

'I do not seek, I find!' The painter Pablo Picasso made that boast. Pai Chang would have approved. For mere seekers he felt only pity. Buddha personifies pure wisdom, it may be, but purity is only visible to the pure. It did not require more than a moment or two for Pai Chang to be quite sure that the blunt and bland pilgrim before him was not likely to achieve Buddha-hood soon. 'I did not come here to edify slobs, but to encourage sages,' was Pai Chang's personal conviction. Pedagogy, as he saw it, consists in pointing out pure things to the pure and impure things to the impure. Hence, the business with the flywhisk. Pai Chang was rude not out of pique but for a purpose, waving a flywhisk at blindness and administering a slight, hardly felt, shock even as he dismissed his interlocutor.

'I am the unworthy fellow who dares to adore the baker's daughter down the hill from here.' There speaks a silly love for sure. 'I am a mirror of the flowers by your doorstep.' There speaks an artist, perhaps, although painters are seldom eloquent. 'I am the Fuller Brush Representative.' There speaks a trained salesman. 'I am your vicar.' Same thing. 'I am your smiling Buddha.' There speaks a liar or a nut of some kind. 'I'm Yang, from the Yangtze, and I have a question or two for you.' There, from Pai Chang's viewpoint, spoke an illusion-trammelled idiot. The poor chap knocked himself out in the first round. Yet he was a far more prophetic figure than Pai Chang himself, and soon due to inherit the whole earth. Indeed, all science-minded, heavy-foot folk, who soberly extrapolate foregone conclusions from the facts at hand, resemble the pilgrim whom Pai Chang turned away. They are numberless, whereas Pai Chang's descendants (of whom I am one) comprise a vanishingly small lunatic fringe today. Face it, why not, and be happy!

When I visit Shinto shrines and Zen gardens, for instance, I go wandering about as in a dream. The Japanese themselves, and not just foreign tourists, push past me uncomprehendingly;

while the guards keep a sharp eye out in case I mean to plant a bomb. Inscrutable *gaijin*, I seem to them. In the past, for aeon after aeon, imagination remained the leading edge of consciousness. But now, no more. Inquiring reporter Yang shoves artists from the gate of the mysterious garden, and kicks misty-eyed romancers downhill.

In rueful recognition of all this, Masao Abe spends much of his time re-casting Buddhist thought in relatively logical modern moulds. More power to that kindly man. Meanwhile, what the hell am I doing here? A good question, although the posh photographer who put it to me the other day did so out of sheer annoyance. He had expected me to leap out of range the moment he came along and cocked his Nikon at a stone lantern. I failed to jump, as usual. Bitingly, he explained that he was on assignment from the *National Geographic*. Then came the cruncher: he asked what my occupation might be.

Zazen? Never heard of it.

The thing to do, Abe tells me, is just sit still until I drop both body and mind. Centuries since, Dogen did that, and he showed others how it can be done. The *zazen* tradition continues strong. Success is always possible, for any individual. Agreed, yet surely things must have been simpler in Dogen's day, before we had electro-chemical-robotic-behaviour-patterns and producer-consumer-profiles, and suchlike wampum to get rid of as well. The sciences have mainly served to multiply man's bright burden of shells . . .

This morning's card which the Reverend Song Ryong sent came at a low moment; it was good to get. 'Entering fire, he is not burned,' Song Ryong wrote, quoting a Taoist text. 'Entering water, he is not drowned.' Gold in the white heat of a crucible, or the moon's reflection, or unattached thought, do all right. I visited Katsura in the rain this afternoon. It was raining on the pond, the fishes' roof, as it is now on mine. The fish flowed and flickered like coloured candle flames under the quicksilver coinage of the rain. Later I did *zazen* while listening to the same thing, feeling it glisten round the grey folds of my brain. Passions, vibrations, rhythms, time itself, all interlock, all interlink, like the ripples which raindrops make, swelling, circling, crossing, and collapsing back again into the surface of a waterlily pond. The point of the whole panorama, however, is just the moment still, as the Japanese poet Basho knew. He wrote:

> Old pond
> Frog plop in
> Listen

A man named Daiju was fortunate enough to find a true teacher of Zen. The teacher, however, simply ignored Daiju for months on end. Daiju made no complaint, but he developed a hangdog manner. One day the teacher lost all patience with him, and shouted: 'What do you want?'

'Enlightenment,' Daiju replied at once.

'You have your own store of light-giving crystals. Why search further than this?'

'Where is it?' But even as he framed the question, Daiju knew. The self whom he so desperately desired to enlighten was already bulging with treasures which were not his to possess in any permanent sense. Moreover there was plenty of illumination there, buried in the treasure. Thus, Daiju awakened, and scattered those 'light-giving crystals' abroad like a sneeze.

Leviathan

Along the steep flank of a glacier, miles above the world, I climbed. The burden of books strapped to my back was terrible. I slipped and fell. 'What not to write', I thought as I was scrambling up again, 'is something I must ask my Guardian Angel.' I clutched one of her wings, and startled the Angel away. A few of her feathers froze to my numb fingers as she soared free. 'What not to write', I repeated to the vast silence of the icy slope, 'should long since have become a burning question.'

My coat hung stiff with quilted colours. It seemed heavier than iron. Again I slipped; the wind caught at its hem to tumble me. Then I was rolling down the glacier like a broken icicle. 'What not to write,' I thought, still clutching for a turn of phrase as the abyss opened below. The green ice melted as I fell, and now the ocean covered me . . .

She had blue-black, long and full, electrically glistening hair, and this enfolded the hollow of my lap like a Mongol tent; while, within the concealment of her tapestried skirt, her snowy bare bottom snuggled my bare toes. For an hour we sat like that, silent in the midst of a throng, in speechless communion; sleeping and waking by turns.

What did it mean? We never met again, so far as I know. Her face was hidden . . .

Rocking into *Dinah*, towards the end, he leaned way over backwards as in the days of his youth. Holding his clarinet out straight, letting it weave just a bit, he seemed to rise right off the floor and yet at the same instant to recline, and blew long drawn-out soul-kisses, and stirred black seed with silver seed in frostbuckets of nitrogen. Sleep-walking, Benny might have been, like the cicada ignorant of death. When he finally finished, the hall rang with appreciative shouts: *Banzai! Banzai!*

His limousine waited at the stage door. Rain streamed in its headlights as we got in. The car pulled away up the alley towards the main street. Near the corner it swerved and skidded to one side. Someone had stepped out of the shadows and signalled our driver to stop. It was a Japanese gentleman, unsmiling and erect. He stepped around to Benny's side of the car. Rolling down the car window, Benny leaned out anxiously. Despite the driving rain, the gentleman removed his hat: 'Mister Goodman, I respect you. I have been waiting to tell you so.'

'Say! Thanks!' As best he could from his seated position, Benny bowed.

Without another word, the stranger turned away and vanished in the streaming darkness. Benny rolled his window up again as we drove on. He was glowing: 'You want to know something? I think that fellow made my night!'

The richly coloured lights of the Ginza flowed like tropical fish around the car. 'You had the applause of thousands,' I reminded him, 'back in the hall.'

'That's right. Confusing, isn't it?'

Yes, the human condition . . .

In Athens, at the Hotel Grande Bretagne, some years ago I met a warty, wary-looking man of middle age. His masklike face was thick with worry and wine. I took him for a professor, perhaps of Soviet studies. But he turned out to be a celebrated psychoanalyst, Jules Masserman. After two or three minutes of small talk, he said:

'Excuse me for presuming on so short an acquaintance, but I can see from your eyes that you have suffered a serious blow to the thorax recently. Perhaps a traffic accident? I am guessing that somebody braked hard in front of you, and that when you regained consciousness you were honking the horn of your car with your heart. Now, have you yet consulted a doctor about the pain which keeps on?'

'No,' I said, wonderingly. 'In fact I've told no one about it.'

'Come upstairs for a moment', Masserman said, 'and let me look at you.'

Upstairs in his hotel suite, after examining my chest and listening to my heartbeat, Masserman straightened smiling. 'Your heart is still in the right place,' he assured me. 'I wanted to be certain, however.' With that, we returned to the party.

Later on that same evening, I noticed Masserman rise from his chair and dart across the room to whisper something in a woman's ear. She stood, waveringly, and he led her away. In half an hour he was back again. 'Incipient hysteria,' he remarked to me. 'I've put her under sedation for the time being. I'll look into her problem later on, towards morning, when she returns to consciousness, but already I believe I have an inkling . . .'

'When do you rest?' I asked.

He shrugged: 'I'm a doctor, don't forget. It's just my job. There are no altruists in this world, you know. We only pretend to virtue, in order to adjust.'

'Adjust to what?'

'Solitude!' From his blind spot, Masserman shot me a sorrowful, defiant look . . .

Cogito – 'I think' – is not strictly accurate. 'I am thought' comes closer to personal experience. How about breathing, then? Breath is life to our physical selves. To say 'I breathe' is factual enough and yet not quite true in a larger sense. What happens is that breath flows in and out of us, and we experience this. Again our minds breathe ideas, as it were. Like the carp and goldfish at Katsura, our non-physical selves swarm flashing through the depths of a single, unfathomable Mind. So, we are not alone. Then why persist in our pretensions to consistency? What is a systematic, well-worked-out philosophy of life? What is a self-contained, conventional self-portrait or autobiography? Fish on a plate. I would rather talk about the fish that got away.

Long before the flood, Hindus relate, Manu the Lawgiver stooped down to wash his hands in the Stream of Beginnings. As he did so, something supple, cool and quick darted between his fingers. Instantaneously clasping it, he lifted the silvery creature out of the water. But air was not its element. The thing gasped through its gills, blinked its opalescent eyes, and wriggled painfully, seared by the warm fingers of the god. With a gesture of compassion, Manu released his catch. The fish turned underwater, rose again, and spoke:

'O, Manu, I am Jhasa, whose destiny it is to rule the deep. Ages hence, when your beard has become grey like my gills, the waters will rise up to cover all the land. But have no fear, Manu, for I promise to take you on my back in that far-distant time, and save you.'

Legend is all one and the same, unfathomably flowing. For example, old Irish chronicles tell how Saint Brendan was accosted by a great fish which announced itself as 'Jastoni'. This happened in the far North Atlantic, where white blizzards shove mountainous green icebergs around. Courteously, the fish invited Brendan to take refuge on its scaly back. The saint did so. He celebrated Easter, Jesus' Resurrection, astride the dorsal fin of the Lord of the Deep.

Jhasa, Jastoni, Leviathan, the many-named gazes up out of unfathomable depths. Glittering, he surfaces to look upon the land, on love and hate, fame and obscurity, knowledge and ignorance. He contemplates experience. And afterwards, down in the calm dark reaches of the ocean, he dreams of what he has witnessed. Then, satisfied, the monster rises again to cavort upon the ridges of the waves, tirelessly. His fiery-phosphorescent wake hemstitches nature. The seemingly irreducible chronon and the roomy Platonic Year are both as one to this ace-in-the-ocean.

Manu, look well; and Brendan, don't forget. This daemon of the sea was born to save you – not your legendary flesh and bones, but you – out of the Deluge which must come.

Stories

Listen, and I will tell you a story concerning our first ancestor. Various powers, angels, demiurges – call them what you like – created Adam in a spirit of play, like children making a snowman. Meanwhile the real First Man, who lives in heaven and who possesses the capacity for expressing himself freely, imparted a secret gift to the image below. To Adam, in other words, because the First Man saw that Adam had been shaped in his likeness. So, Adam suddenly awakened, and opened his mouth, and uttered words. Adam began to name the things of creation, from within.

If a mere statue of a deity, deliberately fashioned by human hands, were to suddenly arise and stride forth from the sculptor's studio, and assert its own authority over creatures of flesh and blood, the priest and artists and all true believers alike would be stricken with panic. For who could possibly expect, let alone welcome, the actual here and now kingship of a heavy marble or bronze idol? The case of Adam and his creators was like this. When Adam first spoke and unburdened himself of what was in his heart – as the angels themselves were unable to do – heaven trembled; tragedy was the result. The angels, being terrified, attacked and badly damaged their own work.

That is only a story, true. So it has always been. So it will be, until we learn and employ an alphabet totally new. Eventually, this challenge must be met. We will have to develop vowels and consonants which manifest themselves not to the ear, nor to the eye, nor to any physical sense whatsoever, but only to the understanding heart alone.

Such an alphabet would convey nothing whatsoever untrue – meaning the end for story-telling? Not at all. It would mean the end of unbelief in stories.

This morning's dream began in heaven. I was a child with a child companion, wandering hand in hand about a high city of light, happy through and through. There was a sort of elevator to the citadel. We stepped in together; the floor went down instead of up; my companion leapt out again but I could not. Alone now, I went down and down to a different city. The doors opened; I wandered out alone. It was a replica of the city of light, but sunken slate, and I was solitary, never to return.

Even to think about the dream, hours later now, makes me shudder. What a coward I am!

Heaven and hell are here, together, this much at least I should know. The elevator has no floor. I am my own companion in this solitude. Aloneness is an illusion. This sufferer I call myself, cut off and separated from the world, is really nothing more than a dirty dry toe-nail paring from my true body – which is not a self but a locus of motion and of rest. A true body is like a beggar-monk, or possibly a pair of them, or even three beggar-monks making their rounds as one.

In fact what woke me was the bee-loud drone of beggar-monks, welling from the narrow street below my window over there. I slid back the window to watch them coming into view with their hats like wide baskets upside-down, their black robes, and their soggy hemp sandals trudging through the mist. They resembled figures in a *sumie* ink-painting, a smudged white scroll. The first in line felt my gaze penetrate his hat. Expressionless, he glanced up. I bowed in greeting. He grinned, and passed pauselessly on below . . .

In the dream-time, a man entered his brother's house with a question. 'This house appears to be quite solid, plain and sensible in all respects but one,' he began. 'However, I do not at all understand these windows which open right onto the public lane. They seem deliberately designed in such a manner as to permit you to observe the people passing by outside, practically within touching distance, and for them to observe you in turn. Yet I notice you keep the curtains drawn, which appears to negate the whole meaning and purpose of having windows in the first place. So, tell me, why is this?'

'I am waiting,' the man's brother explained. 'Some day there will come this way the young mother of our children to be, a girl as yet unknown to me, and she and I will simultaneously open these curtains for the first time, so that light floods in from each window, and every person who passes by will be our friend. Now do you understand?'

'No, not at all. Because, in the first place, you have no way of ascertaining when, if ever, the person for whom you are waiting will actually arrive here. Since these curtains are to remain closed meanwhile, you will not even be aware of the girl if she does appear. In the second place, assuming that she comes at all, and that by some miracle you are able to recognize her presence through these curtains, still you and she never can open the curtains simultaneously as you hope. Why not? Because you are shut inside here, behind the curtains and the dusty glass, while she presumably will be standing or walking by outside, beyond the wall, in open air. Furthermore, if she actually is to become the mother of your children as you hope, then she must be a physical being, an altogether human girl. Such a creature cannot reach in through glass or stone to pull aside a curtain. So, please be reasonable. Remember that this house which you have built and in which we are talking together now is real, solid, actual. What you yourself create with your own hands is objectively acceptable. However, your hopes and dreams exist – if they may

133

be said to have the dignity of some dim wavering existence at all – in some altogether different realm, which must remain peculiar to yourself alone. Confuse these two things, and you deliberately invite frustration of the most galling sort. Worse, people will say that you are touched in the head, a little mad. You had better not expect their friendship, now that I think of it. Keep the curtains as you have them. Keep them so and, finally, forget the girl. This is my considered advice to you.'

The brothers' names were Cain and Abel.

My mother was a marvellous story-teller. She used to carry me by moonlight through the small waves of the forest roof, sailing a feather boat. Yet for her the journey was not all that easy, and now where is she?

There was a man so fortunate as to spend his childhood in the kingdom of joy; and there, like every child, he was a prince of the realm. His parents loved him very much, of course, and they had made a purple robe to his measure. His father provided the fleece for this; his mother spun the thread and wove it on a loom of stone. Yet the time came when they removed the robe from him and sent him down into a strange land, dark and wet. He went bearing treasure with which to pay his way, in his own body. Silver of Gazzak and gold of Ellaie and rubies of Kushan were his feet and hands. The boy was still very young to be so equipped, and often stumbled on his way down through Maishan, Babel, Sarbug, and Egypt, to the dwelling place of the Serpent in the sea. But that loud-humming Serpent lulled the boy into sleep and slavery, so that he soon forgot from whence he came, and then, for three times seven years he served the Serpent faithfully. What was it that released him? A letter, or an eagle, or a broken seal brought the man to himself – for he was now a man – and the freedom in him longed to be free again. Thereupon without delay he stripped off the Serpent's livery, and parted from the palace where he had served. But the Serpent gave him a pearl, a small thing beyond all price or reckoning of worth, to take away. He passed inland by Sarbug and Babel, on his return journey, until he reached the Eastern

Ocean and Maishan, the haven of merchants. There came emissaries from the heights beyond to greet the man, bearing with them the purple robe which his parents had made. He had forgotten that garment.

Yet now, as he faced it, the robe was a dark mirror of himself. He saw his whole self there. The robe and he were two, yet one and the same. The sign of the One was in that bright embroidered robe, with its beryls and agates varied in colour, and it gleamed like the within of a sapphire. Throughout its folds, he saw, the motions of knowledge were stirring, as if to speak. It reached in his direction, spreading itself out upon the wind, and he too was running to meet and receive the robe.

This I believe.

Because, not long ago, when I was walking in the hills east of Kyoto, I came across a small pagoda (which was deserted just then at the stillest hour of afternoon) and there I finally received the first beginning of enlightenment. A patch of sunlight lay across the pagoda step; goldenly inviting it seemed. I made myself comfortable on the step; my body took the *zazen* posture almost automatically. Thinking of nothing in particular, I listened to the birds converse from tree to tree. Their cries were shrill, unmusical, and like the squeak of cleaning-wax energetically applied.

'That's it!'

One of the birds made the comment, sharply, inside my head. At that moment, I vanished from the scene. Where self had been, nothing. I was home. When I returned, or rather when my self returned, the birds had long since flown. The sun was going, too. My spine felt unbendable, rigid with ache. My legs were like wood for a time. I got to my feet, however, and shakily bowed low in the four directions. Then I turned and bowed to the pagoda step which had supported my weight. And finally, with no feeling of foolishness, I blew a farewell kiss to the setting sun. Why?

It was happiness. One hand clapping, and gratitude the other hand.

Zen-Buddhism never calls for murder or for suicide, nor does Christianity. Neither does any genuine philosophy. But sacrifice of self is needed, one way or another. When ego walks out of the door, *satori* may fly in at the window; I know this now. At the pagoda that afternoon, who had forsaken whom?

What I am remains the same, but this does not mean I will be the man in ruins before me.